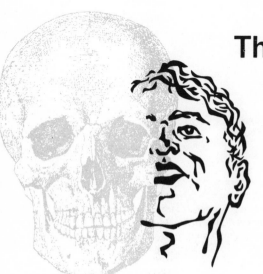

The Concept of Culture

LESLIE A. WHITE
University of California
Santa Barbara

with

BETH DILLINGHAM
University of Cincinnati

Burgess Publishing Company • Minneapolis, Minnesota

Copyright © 1973 by Burgess Publishing Company
Printed in the United States of America
Library of Congress Catalog Card Number 72-88749
SBN 8087-2333-2

2   3   4   5   6   7   8   9   0

Preface

In 1961 I was invited to lecture for two weeks in the Summer Institute of Anthropology for College Teachers at the University of Colorado, Boulder, by Professor Jack Kelso, the Institute's Director. The Institute was sponsored by the National Science Foundation and was designed to offer college teachers an intensive review of the various fields of anthropology for ten weeks. There were thirty-four participants in the Institute in the summer of 1961.

It was hoped that all the lectures of the visiting instructors would be tape-recorded, transcribed, and prepared for publication in a single volume. This hope was not realized, however. My eight lectures were tape-recorded and transcribed, but since the plan for publication had to be abandoned, nothing further was done with them.

About a year ago Dr. Beth Dillingham read these lectures and felt that they would be useful for courses in colleges and universities. We both felt, however, that they should be revised so that they would read like written essays rather than as oral presentations in the first person. Dr. Dillingham undertook to make these revisions, and in doing so she has improved the text in other respects. She has also supplied bibliographic information on many of the points touched upon in the lectures.

The lectures were presented under the rubric "Ethnological Theory," but they were devoted primarily to the concept of culture and to the science of culture; they included, also, some discussion of evolutionism and anti-evolutionism in the nonbiological field of anthropology. They were designed to orient students, both in anthropology and in other fields, in the science of culturology — which dates from the publication of Gustav Klemm's *Allgemeine Culturwissenschaft*, Leipzig, 1854-55, but is still relatively new in the family of sciences. We have supplied copious references to guide the reader to further exploration of this field.

I wish to express my deep appreciation to Professor Kelso for his hospitality and for the tape recordings and transcriptions of the lectures. And to Dr. Dillingham my gratitude, not only for her excellent editing of the lectures, but also for the stimulus that led to their publication.

May, 1972   Leslie A. White
Visiting Professor of Anthropology
University of California, Santa Barbara

Contents

The Basis of Culture: The Symbol

Man is an animal. But he is not "just another animal." He is unique. Man, alone among all species, has an ability which, for want of a better term, we call the ability to symbol. The ability to symbol is the ability freely and arbitrarily to originate, determine, and bestow meaning upon things and events in the external world, and the ability to comprehend such meanings. These meanings cannot be grasped and appreciated with the senses. For example, holy water is not the same thing as ordinary water. It has a value that distinguishes it from ordinary water, and this value is meaningful and significant to millions of people. How does ordinary water become holy water? The answer is simple: human beings bestow this meaning upon it and determine its significance. This meaning can be comprehended by other human beings, of course; if this were not so it could have no significance for them. Symboling, therefore, involves the comprehension of meanings as well as originating and bestowing them.

But, as we have noted, the meanings involved in symboling cannot be grasped and appreciated with the senses. One cannot distinguish holy water from ordinary water with the sense of taste, smell, sight, or touch; nor can the distinction be made by any method of physical or chemical analysis. Nevertheless, the distinction is real; one should not be so naive as to dismiss such things as mere figments of the imagination and, therefore, unreal. After all, nothing is more real than a hallucination.

Let us proceed with a few more examples of symboling, or products of symboling. I obtained from a Pueblo Indian a calcite concretion; at least this is what the geologist said it was. But it was not just a calcite concretion. It was the embodiment of supernatural power; it was a source of supernatural power which the Indians could draw upon and use to *do* things. It was not, then, just a mineral object; it was a fetish also, and as such it had real meaning to the Indians. Here again one could not grasp, or comprehend, its meanings with the senses or by any method of mineralogical analysis. The Indians had freely and arbitrarily bestowed meaning upon it. And the ability to create and bestow nonsensory meanings is also the ability to comprehend them.

1

Meaning can be bestowed upon acts. "Dost you bite your thumb at us?" asks a character in *Romeo and Juliet* (Act I, Scene 1). What does this gesture mean? Whatever its meaning may have been, it was not intrinsic in the gesture itself; it had been bestowed upon it. And, as in the cases of holy water and fetish, the meaning cannot be grasped with the senses.

Symboling can find expression in colors as well as in objects and acts. Red may be the color of a "badge of courage," or of noncapitalist ideology and social organization. Black is not of necessity the color of mourning; among some of the aborigines of Australia, white was the proper color for this occasion.

Meaning may be freely and arbitrarily bestowed upon sounds, upon permutations and combinations of sounds, and upon marks representing these sounds. Thus we have articulate speech and alphabetic writing, respectively. What does the combination of sounds *see* mean? The answer is, nothing intrinsically. But it may mean anything: an optical act; the jurisdiction of a bishop; or, as in the Spanish language, *yes*. In still another language it might mean "the toe-nail of a fox," "milk a sheep," "in a lying position," or anything else. A certain animal may be called *dog* in one language, *perro* in another, *dee-ya* (Keres) in another, as of course we know. There is no intrinsic or necessary relationship between the object on the one hand, and the sounds with which it is designated on the other.

We can coin words: *doko*. What does *doko* mean? It does not mean anything in and of itself, but we can make it mean anything we want to: "the seed of a grape," "tug the lobe of your left ear with the thumb and index finger of your left hand," "oblong in shape," or "all Caucasian men who have red hair, vote the Democratic ticket, play the clarinet, and have an aversion for eggplant." "Words mean just what I want them to mean," Humpty Dumpty told Alice with some emphasis, "nothing more, nothing less." And so it is with all languages: the meanings of words, spoken or written, are not inherent in them and therefore cannot be comprehended with the senses. Meanings have been freely and arbitrarily bestowed upon them and can be comprehended only by man's symboling faculty.

We have, then, a class of phenomena — things, acts, sounds, colors, etc. — that are the products of a kind of behavior: symboling. It is this class of things and events that distinguishes man from all other living species; these phenomena constitute the materials of which all civilization, all cultures, are composed. Yet science has no name for them, which is a very remarkable fact in view of the inveterate habit of science to classify and to name things. The reason for this is, in all probability, that the sciences of man — and of man as a human being — are still young, immature, and have not grappled with fundamentals at some points. But we *need* a name for this all-important class of phenomena, and symbolate has been proposed as a fitting and appropriate name (White, 1959a:231). This was done with some diffidence and even trepidation because coining terms is a risky business: sometimes they bring down ridicule upon one's head (as happened in coining the word *culturology*); or such an offspring may be stillborn, or die in infancy (as in the case of J.W. Powell's *sophiology* or L.H. Morgan's *Ganowanian* family). But in coining this term I have been guided by precedent: if the product of isolating is an *isolate*, why would not the product of symboling be a *symbolate? Symbolate* may be defined as a product of symboling, or a thing or event dependent upon symboling.

It may be asked, why use the word *symboling* instead of *symbolizing?* Does not symbolizing mean the same thing? No, it does not. Symbolizing means "to represent. . .by a symbol; as a nimbus enclosing a cross symbolizes Christ." This meaning is well established by usage. The meaning of "to symbol" is quite different: it means, as we have seen, "to originate, determine and bestow meanings upon things and events, and to comprehend these meanings." These meanings are nonsensory. Therefore symboling is trafficking in nonsensory meanings. Symboling is a kind of behavior (White, 1962), and up to now science has had no name for it. It may well be, of course, that *symboling* is not the best, or the most appropriate, name for this kind of behavior; but so far no better one has been proposed. We have chosen symbol (rather than to coin an entirely new word, such as *totak*, for example) because it is already a well-established word in the English language; therefore there is not so much risk of its being misunderstood or dying as there would be with a new word like *totak*. Furthermore, symbol already has a meaning that is *related to* the phenomenon we are concerned with. And, it is a common practice in the English language to use a word both as noun and as verb: hammer, rope, water, comb, etc. We even have "he flied to left field" and "Quaker State your car." So, in using the word symbol as a verb we are not doing violence to any process in the English language.

At this point the question arises: "What about the ability to symbol among rats and chimpanzees? There are many instances in which reputable psychologists describe the behavior of these animals in terms of symbols." It is true that some psychologists do use the terms "symbol" and "symbolic ability" in describing the behavior of some nonhuman animals. These so-called symbols are such things as green triangles to which white rats respond, or the red and blue poker chips which an ape uses in the "Chimp-o-mat" experiments. However, these are not, technically speaking, *symbols* but *signs*.

A *sign* is a thing that indicates something else: black clouds are a sign of rain; mammalian footprints in my hen house mean that a predator has been there; a yellow quarantine flag is a sign of infectious disease, and so on. There are two kinds of signs: (1) those with meanings inherent in them and their respective contexts, as in the cases of the storm clouds and the preda-

3

tor's footprints, above; and (2) those whose meanings are not intrinsic in them as in the case of the quarantine flag. In the former case, the meanings are, of course, comprehended with the senses: I see the footprints and they are those of a fox, not of a chicken. But in the latter case, also, the meanings are grasped with the senses: the rat distinguishes the red triangle from the green one; the chimpanzee, the red poker chip from the blue one with his optical apparatus. The meanings of *signs* are comprehended with the senses; the meanings of *symbols* are not.

But, one might argue, the meanings of some signs are not inherent in them any more than they are in symbols. What, then, is the difference between the green triangles and the red poker chips, on the one hand, and words (as symbols) on the other?

It is true that the meanings of the green triangles and red poker chips are not inherent in their physical structures. But, they have become identified with their respective physical forms through experience and may thus be comprehended with the senses. We create the word *doko* and assign to it the meaning "jump." At the outset this meaning cannot be grasped with the senses any more than the Aztecs could comprehend *santo* in the speech of the Spanish conquerors with their senses. But, after repeated usage, the meaning of *doko* becomes identified with its physical form and thereafter may be grasped with the senses: we distinguish *doko* from *poko*. "Did you say pig or fig?" the Cheshire Cat asked Alice; he did not hear very well. Symbols become signs through experience, as a consequence of repeated usage.

(We might have pointed out before that a symbol is a composite of two things: a meaning and a physical structure, i.e., an object, an act, a color, or a sound. The physical form or structure is the vehicle by means of which the meaning is transmitted. A symbol must have a physical structure; otherwise it could not enter our experience, unless we are willing to grant the premises of telepathy. But, in symboling, the physical structure of the symbol is perceived; the meaning is not.)

In habitual (repeated) behavior of human beings words function as signs rather than as symbols. "Halt" is a sign to a soldier as "Whoa" is to a horse, or green triangles may be to a white rat, or red poker chips to a chimpanzee. Their meanings are comprehended with the senses.

There is another fundamental difference between the symbols of man and the signs of the rat and chimpanzee. It is true, of course, that the meanings of the green triangles and the red poker chips are not inherent in them; it is true that the meanings of the latter are created and bestowed upon them in a free and arbitrary manner. However, it is not the rat nor the chimpanzee that does the creating and the bestowing; it is the experimenter who does this. Rats and chimpanzees *can acquire such meanings, but they cannot originate and bestow them*. The difference is fundamental.

4

"Dogs can understand words and phrases," as Darwin observed (1871: ch.3). And indeed they can. Little Gua, the baby chimpanzee in the Kelloggs' experiment (Kellogg and Kellogg, 1933) knew and understood more words and phrases at one point in the experiment than did the baby Kellogg boy, Donald. But dogs and apes understand words as *signs*, not as *symbols*.

If a reputable scientist wishes to use the word *symbol* in describing the behavior of rats and chimpanzees is he wrong? Does he not have as much right to use this word in this way as we do in another way? Of course he "has a right" to use *symbol* as he pleases. The meanings of words are not inherent in them; they are determined, established, by usage. But if he uses the word *symbol* to describe the behavior of nonhuman animals, what term would he use to designate that which is peculiar and unique to man? We are confronted by two fundamentally different kinds of behavior, one in which meanings are comprehended by nonsensory means, the other in which they are comprehended with the senses. We need words to distinguish these two kinds of behavior, and we use *symbol* and *sign*, respectively, for this purpose.

This brings us to another question: is a word a symbol or a sign? The answer is that it all depends. Is a Navaho rug a scientific specimen, an article of commerce, or a work of art? A Navaho rug is a Navaho rug. It becomes a commodity in one context, a scientific specimen in another. And so it is with words. A word is a word. In one context, in one kind of behavior, a word functions as a symbol; in another, it functions as a sign. It is a matter of context, not of the thing itself.

What makes it possible for man to symbol? Why cannot apes symbol? Is the answer to be found in the size or structure of their respective brains? The answer is that we know almost nothing about the neuroanatomy of symboling. No examination of the brains of men and apes so far has been able to tell us why the former can symbol and the latter cannot. Inasmuch as man is characterized by an extremely large brain, absolutely and relatively, as compared with the ape, and inasmuch as the forebrain is especially well developed in man, we may reasonably assume that these facts are very relevant to the ability to symbol. But this tells us very little indeed. About all we can say now is that the process of evolution in general, and the evolution of the nervous system in particular, among primates eventually produced the neurological mechanism of symboling.

Although we know very little about the anatomy of symboling, we know a great deal about the behavioral antecedents of symboling. We are able to trace the evolution of minding from its lowest level among the earliest and simplest organisms through successive stages until we reach the level of symboling in man. And this helps us greatly to understand the process by which the ability to symbol was developed. Since we have traced this evolutionary process in an essay (White 1960) we shall not repeat or summarize it here.

What can we say about the transition from pre-man to man, from a non-symboling, uncultured primate to a symboling, cultured primate? First of all, we must note that symboling was nonexistent among all forms of life on this planet until man appeared; at least, we have no evidence of it prior to the appearance of man. Man's immediate prehuman ancestors were incapable of symboling (by definition). Was the transition to symboling gradual, or sudden and abrupt? We are obliged to say that it was sudden. There are no degrees of symboling; an organism is either capable of symboling or it is not; there are no intermediate stages between non-symboling and symboling. There are, of course, many changes that are sudden and abrupt in nature: the hatching of a bird, the birth of a placental mammal (the severing of the umbilical cord), the freezing of water, the evaporation of water, and so on. So, we must think of a long process of the evolution of the primates, especially in its neurological aspects, until a certain threshold was reached: the maturation of the ability to symbol. And when this point was reached, it could, and would, be expressed fully and in a variety of forms: in speech, gesture and act, and in objects.

We can observe a transition from a pre-symboling stage to that of symboling today in infants of the human species. A baby is not able to symbol at birth nor during the first months of infancy. It has the *potential* ability to symbol, but this potentiality is not realized until the baby is many months old. Then, when a certain threshold is reached in the course of his development, the ability to symbol is sufficiently matured to find overt expression in behavior. The change is, relatively speaking, sudden and abrupt. In the experiment of the Kelloggs referred to above (1933) much attention was given to the question of articulate speech. Much effort was expended in an attempt to teach the little chimpanzee to talk. But the result of this was not that she made very little progress; she made absolutely none at all. Donald, the infant *Homo sapiens*, was unable to talk, too, during the early months of the experiment, and was even inferior to the younger ape in the comprehension of words and phrases as signs. But, when Donald reached a certain age, his potential ability to symbol was realized and expressed in overt behavior. From that point on he made rapid progress in becoming humanized, while Gua remained on the nonhuman level.

The case of Helen Keller is also instructive. Helen was rendered totally deaf and blind by disease in infancy. As a child she was cut off, isolated, from human beings by her deafness and blindness. At the age of seven she was not a human being from the standpoint of kind of behavior. She was unable to use her potential ability to symbol. She could communicate by means of signs, but not with symbols. She could not employ articulate speech. She was excluded from the whole world of human concepts, meanings, ideals, values, and acts. Then, thanks to the skill and patience of Ann Sullivan, the teacher who was engaged to teach Helen, Helen was enabled to effect contact with the world of human beings through articulate speech, through symboling, and she became a human being. The transition was not merely sudden and abrupt; it was virtually instantaneous. Her diary, and that of Miss Sullivan, give us a most vivid and graphic account of this episode.

Within three weeks of her arrival Miss Sullivan had taught Helen eighteen nouns and three verbs, spelling them out in her hand. Helen confused the word signs for "mug" and "water" because, apparently, both were associated with drinking. In an attempt to clear up this confusion, Miss Sullivan took Helen out to the pump in the garden. In Miss Sullivan's words:

I made Helen hold her mug under the spout while I pumped. As the cold water gushed forth, filling the mug, I spelled "w-a-t-e-r" into Helen's free hand. The word coming so close upon the sensation of cold water rushing over her hand seemed to startle her. She dropped the mug and stood as one transfixed. A new light came into her face. She spelled "water" several times. Then she dropped on the ground and asked for its name and pointed to the pump and the trellis, and suddenly turning round she asked for my name. . .In a few hours she had added thirty new words to her vocabulary. (Keller 1903:316)

Describing the same experience, Helen wrote:

*We walked down the path to the well-house, attracted by the fragrance of the honeysuckle with which it was covered. Someone was drawing water and my teacher placed my hand under the spout. As the cool stream gushed over one hand she spelled into the other the word water, first slowly, then rapidly. I stood still, my whole attention fixed upon the motion of her fingers. Suddenly I felt a misty consciousness as of something forgotten — a thrill of returning thought; and somehow **the mystery of language was revealed to me**. I knew then that "w-a-t-e-r" meant the wonderful cool something that was flowing over my hand. That living word awakened my soul, gave it light, hope, joy, set it free! (Keller 1903:23.)*

Thus, Helen was transformed instantly from a non-symboling creature to a symboling human being.

And so, we may reasonably believe, it was with pre-man and man. For ages before the advent of man the ability to symbol was being developed within the process of neurological evolution. Finally a threshold was reached, and the ability ceased to be potential and was realized in actuality. It was like water being heated gradually until finally it reaches the boiling point. Then it is transformed, suddenly and abruptly, into something else: steam.

Once the ability to symbol was matured and given expression, culture-creating and culture-building commenced. And in a relatively short time, we

7

may justifiably believe, every group of human beings had a complete, though crude, simple, and meager, culture. That is to say, each culture was composed of articulate speech; of beliefs that could be, and were, expressed in speech; and of customs, conventional attitudes, tools, utensils, ornaments, and perhaps clothing. We may form some notion of what the earliest cultures must have been like by observing the most primitive cultures known to science, such as those of the aborigines of Australia and Tasmania (see, e.g., Tylor 1893). Certainly those cultures could hardly have been much more primitive and still remain on the human level. We are not saying, of course, either that the first cultures of mankind were like those of aboriginal Australia in specific detail, or even that they were as highly developed as those of Australia. We are merely saying that the most primitive cultures known to nineteenth century science help us form a realistic picture of the earliest cultures of mankind.

In summary: we have thus far examined man as an animal and man as a human being. We have described and defined that which sets man apart from all other animals. The ability to symbol has been analyzed and illustrated, and it has been distinguished from sign behavior. The consequences of symboling are the humanization of individuals and the origin and development of culture. We shall turn to this subject in our next chapter.

Man and Culture

Man and culture constitute an inseparable couplet. By definition there is no culture without man and there is no man without culture. All definitions are arbitrary. This does not mean, however, that they are not valid, that they are not justifiable, that they are not useful and truthful. But all definitions are arbitrary. They are man-made. Some definitions are better than others. We make, choose and select, and reject definitions on the basis of their adequacy for purposes of scientific explanation. Here we are defining man as a symboling animal, and we define culture in terms of symboling, so that there is no man without culture and no culture without man.

By definition, therefore, culture is brought into being by symboling. Let us for the moment use a rough conception of culture: beliefs, ideologies, social organization, and technology (the use of tools). What about the behavior of animals other than *Homo sapiens*? Why can't we call their behavior culture? Ants have social organization. All animals have social organization. Even plants have social organization. (Plant ecology is plant sociology.) Apes use tools. Beavers build dams. Birds build nests. Radcliffe-Brown (1957:91), speaking about weaver birds building nests, says that if this is learned and transmitted, it is culture.

Certainly some subhuman animals have knowledge and conceptions. The problems solved by Köhler's chimps (1926) involved insight and foresight. (This is an inference drawn by the scientific observer and it is a valid inference.) Apes understand complex things. They know how to use levers. They have knowledge in the sense of being able to behave meaningfully and effectively with reference to things in the external world. In many problem situations apes have a choice of solving problems; and apparently they size up situations and decide upon a certain course of action and try it; if it does not work they will try something else. Why isn't this culture?

The social organization of all nonhuman species is determined biologically. Within a species of bears there are not different kinds of social organization. Social organization in bears is a function of bodily structure, of genetic composition. (Here again this is an inference. But we should not belittle inference, for without inference there would be no science.) In the human species social organization is not a function of bodily structure, but a function of an external suprabiological tradition which we call "culture." Within the human species there is a great variety of social organization. Consequently (and here is a very important point that is often overlooked), there are two fundamentally different kinds of sociology: (1) the sociology of nonhuman species, which is a subdivision of biology, and (2) the sociology of human beings, which is a subdivision of the science of culture, or culturology, because it is a function of this external suprabiological, supraorganic tradition called culture. This is a fundamental difference between the social organization of man and the social organization of all other creatures.

With regard to the use of tools, among insects, for example, it must almost certainly be instinctive, i.e., built into the genetic structure. Beavers and apes apparently have freedom of choice and alternatives. But there is a fundamental difference between the tool processes among subhuman primates and the tool process among human beings. The tool process among subhuman primates is discontinuous psychologically as well as in overt behavior; it is nonprogressive; it is nonaccumulative. The tool process in the human species is a continuous process subjectively (i.e., psychologically) and it is cumulative and progressive. And the difference is due to symboling. The incorporation of tool-using into the symboling (conceptual) process transforms it radically and makes it something very very different.

The social organization of nonhuman species is fundamentally different from that of the human species; and the tool process, also, is fundamentally different. The conceptual process among subhuman species is different because nonhuman animals cannot express concepts overtly in articulate speech. The only way that an ape can express a concept is in terms of behavior. *Homo sapiens* can deal with concepts *as* concepts, manipulate concepts as concepts, which he does in articulate speech. The similarities between culture and nonhuman social organization and tool use which seem to be significant to some people are only superficial similarities. Frequently these similarities conceal a fundamental difference. And nothing is more unfortunate in science than to allow similarities to obscure fundamental differences.

In the long course of biological evolution primates came into being and then man. Man was the product of a biological revolution. Biological change is not merely gradual in evolution; there is revolution too. When a symboling animal was produced by the natural biological processes of evolution and revolution, culture came into being. It came into being as a consequence of the exercise of the ability to symbol. With articulate speech, which is of course the important and characteristic form of symboling, the whole world becomes classified and conceptualized and verbalized; and relationships are established between things on the basis of these conceptions.

For example, chimpanzees have, biologically speaking, uncles and cousins and so on. And these biological relationships are social relationships also. But there is no way to order them without articulate speech. We have a saying "a monkey's uncle," but a monkey does not know who he is. How can one tell an uncle from a cousin without articulate speech? With articulate speech one can classify all biological and social relationships, and this is exactly what takes place in the human species.

Nothing is more impressive among the cultures of some primitive peoples than their kinship systems, where, for example, in a tribe of hundreds of people, everyone is designated by each person with a kinship term, which designates a social relationship. And this social relationship means duties and obligations in the actual conduct of life. So, with articulate speech all persons with whom one has social relations are classified and designated, and duties and obligations are specified for each category. This then constitutes an organization for mutual aid which makes life more secure. Any organism will employ any means at hand to make life more secure; for such behavior has biological survival value for the species. Articulate speech, expressing kinship systems, has been one of the most powerful aids to the survival and progress of man and culture. What is true with respect to kinship systems is true for property and tools, and political and economic systems: they are created, ordered, and regulated by means of articulate speech, by symboling. Thus, an entirely new kind of organization is formed. The social organization of subhuman primates is determined by their body structure, their genetic composition. Although their social organization may be modified in one way or another by external circumstances, these variations fall within a very narrow range. With symboling and articulate speech, however, the door is open for almost infinite variation of organization and development.

With regard to knowledge, the knowledge possessed by prehuman primates is now given verbal expression, and exists not merely in the form of subjective concepts, but is given overt expression in words. This makes for facile and versatile communication. Language also makes possible the storing up of knowledge as well as its transmission. So that symboling and articulate speech create social organization, economic institutions, transform the tool process into a progressive, cumulative process, create a tradition of knowledge and beliefs. And along with this are the ceremonies, rituals, and so on which are created.

Here, of course, are the obvious expressions of symboling. In ritual, symboling is externalized in motion. Rituals, ceremonies, and paraphernalia are some of the purest forms of symboling and some of the most difficult to understand. We do not yet understand many of these rituals, such as the ritual of circumcision or subincision among some societies like the aborigines of Australia. Rituals provide an example of the creation and bestowing of meaning upon things in the external world. As observed above, failure on the part of primitive man and even many civilized people to understand this has led them to invoke a supernatural origin. The supernatural world was created by symboling. Failure to understand this has led to the belief that the supernatural world has an existence independently of the natural world and independently of man, simply because man could not tell the difference between himself and the external world.

How could there be philosophy without articulate speech? How could there be different forms of the family without articulate speech? Or incest rules and taboos? How could one commit adultery without articulate speech? How could an economic system exist without it? How could one distinguish between group property and individual ownership? How could there be chiefs and clans? As a matter of fact, how could there be *anything* in the realm of human social organization without articulate speech? Likewise, without articulate speech there would be no *human* technology. Culture as a whole — ideologically, sociologically, and technologically — is dependent upon symboling as expressed primarily by articulate speech.

Having discussed the origin of culture as a consequence of the exercise of the ability to symbol, we turn now to a discussion of the function of culture. What does it do? What are its functions? The answer is very simple and obvious. The function of culture is to make life secure and enduring for the human species; its function is zoological. Man is an animal as well as a human being. One of the distinctive features of anthropology is that it tries to correlate the biological with the cultural. Nowhere else among our academic disciplines is this effort to correlate the biological and cultural made. (Perhaps anthropology does not do it well, but at least it tries.) The culturologist should never forget the biological dimension of man; and the physical anthropologist should always be aware of the cultural factor because all men live in a cultural environment. So, the function of culture is to serve the needs of man, to make life secure and enduring.

The needs of man can be divided into two classes: those needs which can be satisfied by drawing upon the materials in the external world, and those which can be satisfied without drawing upon the external world. The latter are the psychological and "spiritual" needs. Perhaps we should qualify the phrase "to serve the needs of man" to read "as he conceives of his needs, what he believes to be his needs." The needs that can be satisfied by drawing upon the external world are fairly obvious. Food is essential to life. Other materials are necessary for purposes such as clothing, shelter, locomotion, and so on. Culture as a whole exploits the resources of the external world to provide materials to make life more secure, continuous, and enduring.

Since we have already analyzed culture into ideological, sociological, and technological components, let us add a word about these categories. We make classifications for convenience of analysis, description, explanation, and discussion. In actuality technological elements of culture do not exist as disparate parts of a cultural system, of course. Culture is an integrated whole. Everything is related to everything else in a cultural system. No tool exists apart from social organization, or from ideas and beliefs. Thus, "ideological," "sociological," and "technological" are categories which are logical, useful, and helpful; but they should not be construed as being separate entities. When we say that culture as a whole exploits the resources of nature, we mean that the resources are exploited ideologically, sociologically, and technologically. This seems very plain and therefore should require no further discussion.

We should, however, discuss a little more fully the way in which culture serves inner psychological or spiritual needs. What sort of psychological or spiritual life a gorilla or a raccoon has is unknown. Perhaps it is not possible to identify in a raccoon or a gorilla that which corresponds to the spiritual life of man. It is something that is worth thinking about, and perhaps talking about, however. But certainly with regard to the human species we know a lot about the subject. When we say that man has psychological needs, spiritual needs, we are expressing an inference drawn from our observations of his behavior. One of the tremendously important functions of culture is to satisfy these needs, to give man courage, confidence, morale, comfort, consolation. Every military man, every athletic coach, every prize fighter trainer knows that morale, confidence, and courage are important factors in any contest. The human species has been and is in a contest with other animals, and even within its own species, for survival. It needs courage or guts or spirit and confidence and consolation. Culture provides man with these aids in the form of ideology, ceremonies, and so on. Methods of providing security are enormously elaborated by culture. There has been the belief in Western culture for centuries in the brotherhood of mankind, in mutual aid, in peace. Among early primitive peoples, mythology gave them confidence and assurance. The Jews are not the only chosen people; every people is a chosen people. Every people has its own god to take care of them, and everybody's god is better than anybody else's god. Through the aid of their gods and supernatural power, their rituals, magic, prayer, and ceremonies, primitive peoples can not only control the external world but can also promote social solidarity. One of the consequences of the growth of science is that it has robbed man of this feeling of confidence and of significance in the cosmos. A great deal of spiritual desolation followed in the wake of the growth of science. All of the vicissitudes of life and the uncertainties and tragedies of life can be faced better with the illusions of supernaturalism. There is no way to calculate the extent to which mythologies, rituals, ceremonies, and social organization have contributed to the survival of the human species by providing morale, a feeling of significance, a feeling that life has meaning, is worth living, and by giving comfort and consolation when tragedy does strike.

Let us close this discussion of the functions of culture by again emphasizing the zoological aspect. Culture does serve the needs of man as they are conceived by him. These include spiritual, aesthetic, and temperamental, as well as nutritional and protectional, needs. Man can create and bestow any meaning or value that he wants to. In addition, man, like every other organism, has to evaluate everything. This is very important. Every organism has to evaluate everything in its environment, to distinguish between injurious and beneficial and indifferent. Man does this too, but as a human being he does it by symboling. He determines meaning and value, or at least these meanings and values come to be expressed, in concepts and words. So he says that ice is cold, and water flows, and you can boil water and it will evaporate. He can also say that some water will give eternal life. These are things the gorilla cannot do. A gorilla cannot baptize himself or others. And mules cannot commit suicide because of dishonor. In this process of evaluating things any answer is better than none, because if there is no answer there is uncertainty, apprehension, anxiety, tension, and so on. The human being not only asks questions but can, and must, answer them.

There are several kinds of questions that we can ask about culture, or to put the matter another way, there are a number of ways in which culture can be explained. One question is "How can we account for the origin of culture?" Another question is "What are the functions of culture?" And still another is "How are variations of culture in time, space, and race to be explained?" Let us make clear what is meant by these variations. The culture of mankind is not homogeneous. It is tremendously varied, and these variations have a temporal dimension, for a given culture changes in time. The culture of the United States today is not what it was one hundred years ago. Culture also varies from place to place: the culture of New York State is not the same as the culture of Thailand. And culture varies with peoples: the culture of the Eskimos is not the same as that of the pygmies of Luzon or of the Malay Peninsula. These are the three most important questions that the science of culture would ask about culture: the origin, the function, the variation; and under the latter we have three kinds of variation: with time, place, and peoples.

This brings us to a proposition that is very interesting and very important, but about which there has been a great deal of misunderstanding, disagreement, and controversy. The proposition is this: the human organism, the human species, must be taken into account in discussing the origin of culture and the function of culture; but variations of culture can be, should be, and must be discussed without reference to the human organism. Or to put it another way, the human organism is relevant, not only relevant but necessary, to an explanation of the origin of culture and the function of culture; but it is not even relevant, much less necessary, to an explanation of variations of culture. So that variations of culture with regard to time and place are to be discussed without reference to the human organism. A consideration of the human organism is both relevant and necessary to a discussion of the origin and function of culture, but is superfluous and objectionable in a discussion of variations of culture.

There are a number of anthropologists who object to the proposition that anything meaningful can be said about culture without taking the human organism into account. This notion was repulsive to Ruth Benedict (1934) and to David Bidney (1944); it is also objectionable, evidently, to Radcliffe-Brown (1940;1937), Irving Hallowell (1945), and to many others (see White 1969). This thesis has been refuted repeatedly by the simple statement, "Yes, but you can't have culture without people" — as if anyone thought you could! The proposition that there are important problems in the science of culture which can be solved best by complete disregard of the human organism is regarded by many people as preposterous and ridiculous (e.g., Kardiner and Preble 1961). But that is because they do not understand the science of culture. The curious thing is that many subsidiary propositions that add up to this one are acceptable but not the final conclusion. For example, those who object to an elimination of a consideration of the human organism from certain problems of culturology will admit that if a baby is born and reared in a Tibetan language environment he will speak Tibetan, and that if he is reared in a French language environment he will speak French. They will also admit that one does not need to examine the palate, teeth, tongue, etc., to tell why an individual speaks Tibetan or French; the organs do not have anything to do with it. They will accept these propositions piecemeal, but when the propositions are put together and produce consistent theory, they dissent. We will return to this later. Let us reiterate the first two propositions and return to the third in the next chapter.

The first two propositions are easy and simple. Culture cannot be understood, the actual culture that exists in the real world, without knowing something about man as an animal. The science of culture does not disregard the human organism entirely. An understanding of the origin of culture requires an understanding of man. An understanding of the functions of culture requires an understanding of man. Culture in general is what it is because man in general is the kind of animal that he is. That is a very fundamental proposition in the science of culture. If man were a different kind of animal, the culture of mankind in general would be different. If man did not have stereoscopic and chromatic vision, culture would be different. The culture of the human race is in part a function of the kind of eyes that man has, and if he did not have chromatic vision, culture would be different. Likewise, if he did not have stereoscopic vision culture would be different. As a matter of fact, if ears were not conveniently placed, how could man wear spectacles? There are other ways of holding them on, of course, but the point should be clear. Suppose that the adult male was sixteen feet high or only sixteen inches high. Suppose that the human species could subsist only upon fruit, or only upon cereals, or only upon meats. Suppose we had a breeding season and that babies could be born only in the spring. Our culture would be different. If we reproduced in litters like pigs or puppies, our culture would be different. We would have to have a different kinship terminology. Such examples could be extended indefinitely.

There is an intimate and necessary relationship between man, as a kind of animal, and culture generically, taking culture as a whole. And the origin and function of culture cannot be understood without a great deal of understanding about man. But, when we turn to variations of culture, in time and place, a consideration of the human organism is not only unnecessary, but is an obstruction, an obstacle. Man is necessary for the *existence* of culture but *not for an explanation of its variations*. Many people confuse these two things. Since obviously man is necessary for the existence of culture, many anthropologists think that *all* explanations of culture require a consideration of the human organism. Such is not the case, as we shall see in the succeeding chapter.

Man, Cultural Variation, and the Concept of Culture

With respect to the relationship between man and culture, we have noted that there is an intimate and necessary relationship between culture in general and man in general. When we consider the origin of culture or the function of culture, the nature of the human organism has to be taken into account. But when we deal with specific cultures and their variations, we find no necessary functional relationship between any particular group of persons and any particular culture.

Variations in culture occur with reference to race, or particular groups of people. By "race" we mean a group of people distinguishable from other groups on the basis of biological and physical features. (There is no scientific definition of race that is generally accepted by anthropologists or anybody else.) We find variations of culture in terms of race as well as place and time.

There has been for a very long time a notion that races differ in their culture-building capacities, and even in their innate abilities to receive, to use, or appreciate culture; that these differences are biological, inborn, innate; and that, therefore, some cultural differences are due to biological differences of race. This idea is very old. It is deep-seated in many of our traditions, and it still persists. Over a hundred years ago one of the early pioneers in anthropology, a German named Gustav Klemm, divided the peoples of the world into "active" and "passive" races. The active races were the ones that had the highest cultures according to Klemm's criteria; and the passive races were the ones that had the lower cultures. Many others also have subscribed to this view. About the time of World War I there was a great deal of discussion in the United States about cultures in terms of race. There was much talk of Nordic supremacy, and of how the future of the world rested upon the Nordic race. Even such a competent and distinguished scientist as Clark Wissler had more than one passage in his writings about the light of civilization being carried by the Nordic race.

This belief was supported by some evidence; but many things are supported by evidence that are nevertheless unsound. There is a great deal of evidence to support the belief of primitive peoples that their dances are efficacious in bringing rain: it often rains after a rain dance. The reason it rains is, of course, that they hold their rain dances in the rainy season. Many sick people recover their health after being treated by a medicine man. Thus, real evidence may support a false or invalid proposition.

There was considerable evidence in support of the belief that races differ in their ability, and that the superior races were the ones that produced superior cultures and the inferior races either produced nothing or very little. There was also evidence that some of the inferior races were even incapable of acquiring the higher cultures. For example, a hundred years ago when Lewis Henry Morgan was out in the Great Plains he talked about the Indians with missionaries, traders, and government agents. There was a very widespread belief among these people that the cultures of the Plains Indians were the direct expression of their innate human nature. They would tell Morgan, "You cannot change Indians — they are wild and cannot be domesticated" (Morgan 1959). The fact is that tremendous effort and pressure on the part of white American culture to domesticate the Plains Indians failed, and their cultures stubbornly persisted. Thus, the white man's thesis about the Indians was supported by considerable evidence. As already noted, many unsound propositions may be supported by evidence. But "some evidence" is not enough.

The assertion that peoples possessing superior cultures have superior brains, nerves, and glands is solely an inference. It is a biological inference drawn from culturological data, and in order to validate it one would have to be able to measure biological ability in some other way, directly if possible. No such way has ever been devised. So that at best, it is an inference. There is no *direct* evidence, no direct measure of man's innate ability at all, that would justify this assertion. On the other hand there is a great deal of evidence to show that this inference is unsound. For example, take the North American Indians, who are by and large a fairly uniform physical type (and can therefore be treated as a biological constant) but their cultures differ enormously. Here the picture presents a biological constant with cultural diversity. Some of the most advanced cultures of the world have been possessed by all of the three great major races, Caucasoid, Negroid, and Mongoloid; and some of the lowest cultures of the world have been in the hands of representatives of each of these groups. Thus there is a marked lack of correlation between race and culture.

Furthermore, it is a known fact that the culture possessed by a given physical type or race can and does change through time. People whose ancestors have possessed a very low culture are, under certain circumstances, quite capable of appropriating quite advanced cultures. So, although we have examples of persistences of aboriginal culture among American Indians, we also have many examples of individual Indians, and even groups, that have appropriated American culture quite readily. We conclude, therefore, that there is no direct evidence in support of a theory of biological superiority, or of biological differences in terms of inferiority and superiority in cultural capacity. On the contrary, there is a great deal of evidence against such a theory. The most justifiable view that we now have is that there is no significant correlation between culture and race. There are good reasons to believe that none exists. This is not to say that all races are equal in mental abilities, in temperament, etc. In the absence of an ability to make direct measurements, such a claim is unfounded. But, from the standpoint of explaining cultural differences and variations with reference to physical type, the only sound and safe assumption that we have today is that the biology of man may be regarded as constant. And, of course, variables cannot be explained in terms of constants. In fact, no significant correlation exists between any physical type and any kind of culture.

We turn now to variations with regard to place. Cultures differ with place. Every culture exists in an actual, real habitat. That is perfectly obvious. And there is, and must be, an intimate relationship between any particular culture and its habitat. It is easy, however, to exaggerate the influence of habitat upon culture types. The fact that many cultures show and reflect environmental influence has sometimes led to exaggerated theories of environmental or geographic determinism. The fact that there is some influence has led some scholars to claim that all cultures are determined by geographic and environmental conditions. In criticism of this view, it has been pointed out that we do not always find similar cultures in similar environments. The Eskimo culture shows remarkable adaptation. The culture of the Indians of Tierra del Fuego, who live in an environment comparable to that of the Eskimos, is very different from that of the Eskimos. Here a theory of environmental determinism suffers. One of the best habitats in the world, in terms of climate, vegetation, etc., is that of Tasmania; and yet the culture of the aborigines of Tasmania was probably the crudest known to modern science. Correlations between culture and habitat are not close at all, which leads us to the conclusion that while there is and must be an intimate relationship between every culture and its habitat, within this relationship there is room for much variation. The habitat may permit certain things and prohibit certain others, but there is still room for a great deal of variation.

We have been discussing variation of culture in terms of place. Let us now divide place into two categories: (1) environment, in terms of climate, topography, flora, fauna, and mineral substances, and (2) place as location. The latter is something that is very seldom discussed, at least specifically. But the location of a culture in a big land mass, or with reference to big land masses, or with reference to connecting links between great land masses, may be of enormous significance. This, I believe, might be called the topological dimension of cultural variation. The idea is plain and simple. Suppose there is a great land mass. Other things being equal, the culture in the center has more chance of being highly developed than one on the periphery. This is so because of the contrast between isolation and interaction. Assuming random movement of culture traits, there would be more interaction among them in the center of a land mass than on the periphery, and therefore a greater possibility for recombination of traits in the center. Or suppose there are two great land masses, such as Asia and Africa, or North and South America, with a connecting link between them. Then, assuming random migration and random diffusion, cultures near this link will have a greater chance to grow because a greater amount of interaction will take place there. The areas between Egypt and Mesopotamia and between Mexico and Peru are examples. If all the land of the world were absolutely uniform climatically, topographically, and in the flora and fauna, there would still be differentials with regard to cultural growth due to the actual location of cultures. This factor could be even more significant than the immediate environmental influence since so many cultures do not utilize some of the available resources.

Now we turn to cultural variations in terms of time. If we take the world as a whole, culture as a whole, and divide it into time periods, we find variation within these periods. These variations are usually ascribed to, or interpreted in terms of, cultural development. This is not the whole story, however, because there are cultural variations in terms of time that are not the result of cultural development, but rather are the result of cultural diffusion, of the spreading of culture from one place or people to another. We have then two different kinds of interpretation of cultural variation with regard to time: history and evolution. Suppose, for example, there were in Mesopotamia some cultures that subsisted wholly upon wild food, particularly plant food, but some animal food as well. Then after a period of time, x thousand years later, in the same place there is agriculture. This would be an example of cultural growth or development, of change and advance within itself. (The term advance, or progress, as used here means greater control over the forces of nature through cultural means, so that life is made more secure and enduring for the people in that particular culture. The terms are not subjective value judgments; they are objective and measurable.) In this case we have an example of origin, of the transition from wild food to domesticated food in a certain area. This is an example of cultural variation in time which is introduced by a kind of culture process which we call "evolution."

An example of a different kind of culture change through time is that of the Pueblo Indians of the Southwest before and after 1540, the year in which Coronado visited the region. Coronado's group effected little change in Pueblo culture, but by 1598 there was a colonizing party which caused many changes in Pueblo culture. This type of culture change is not change by evolution; it is change by diffusion. It is more than diffusion, however, because the Spanish not only brought in new traits but did their best to extirpate some Pueblo traits. We have a fairly good documentary record of their attempts to extirpate some of the Pueblo culture traits, so it is really more than mere diffusion. A number of problems in Pueblo ethnology have revolved around the attempt to determine what traits of nineteenth century Pueblo culture were aboriginal and what traits were introduced by the Spanish.

Another example of change by diffusion is the culture of Japan in 1868 and the culture of Japan in 1890. In 1868, the Tokugawa period came to a close. This marked the end of a primitive, isolated, backward culture politically, economically, and technologically. Western technology was introduced and the country was transformed almost overnight. Here is a clear example of culture change through time by diffusion.

Before leaving this subject (to which we will return later), it is of interest to note that among anthropological students of culture there have been a number of emphases, goals, or objectives. Some students of culture have been primarily interested in one objective, some in another. The result has been the formation of schools. The term "school" refers to a group of people who tend to share a common point of view, purposes, goals, and objectives. The history of anthropology discloses a number of schools. They are primarily three in number: (1) the evolutionist school, which is interested in growth, development, evolution; (2) the diffusionist-historical schools, composed of students of culture who have been interested in the variations of culture in time and place and in the spread of culture throughout the world from one place to another in a chronological sequence; and (3) the functionalist school, whose members have been interested in how cultural systems work as such; their problems are nontemporal. (This was called the functional school in the 1930s but it is now called the British structuralist school and also social anthropology. Emphasis has shifted from function to structure, but in all instances structure and function are inseparable.)

At this point we need to turn ourselves directly to a discussion of the concept of culture. Up until now we have been using the term "culture" as a simple, undefined term, a word to designate the beliefs, customs, institutions, art, tools, etc., that all people have. Let us begin our discussion with a history of the concept of culture in anthropology.

The word "culture" was introduced into anthropology and made a technical term by Edward B. Tylor, the British pioneer in this science. In the opening words of *Primitive Culture* (1871) he describes culture as "that complex whole which includes knowledge, belief, art, law, morals, custom and any other capabilities and habits acquired by man as a member of society." Tylor borrowed the term "culture" from the German culture historians. In the intellectual world of western Europe in the nineteenth century, German scholars in particular were interested in what they called "culture." They were mainly interested in culture history and wrote a great deal about it. Gustav Klemm (1802-1867) wrote quite a number of books, one of which was called *Culture History* and another *General Culture History of Mankind.* He was probably the first person to use this phrase.

Tylor's conception of culture (conception, rather than definition, because the words which followed the word "culture" did not constitute a definition) was quite clear, although it was expressed in various places in his writings rather than being included all in one place. Had Tylor had any notion of what would happen in anthropology within the decades after his death, he would undoubtedly have taken pains to be more explicit and specific so as to avoid a lot of the difficulties over the concept that have arisen since his time. Tylor made it clear that culture is that which is peculiar to the human species, and he emphasized the fundamental difference between the mind of man and that of lower animals. He rejected the notion that it is just a matter of degree, that man is just a more talented ape than the gorilla. He made it clear that culture is those nonbiological things that are peculiar to man, things that are transmitted by nongenetic means. This is the conception of culture that Tylor had, and which he bequeathed to his successors.

Cultural anthropology has been cultivated in the Western world primarily by English-speaking people. The concept of culture that Tylor bequeathed to his successors was very useful; it was realistic and unambiguous. The term "culture" was a useful and satisfactory conceptual tool for dealing with the different ways of life that Europeans were coming into contact with. For decades the term "culture" served everyone very well. Tylor's definition was used by Lowie on the first page of his *Primitive Society*, published in 1920. It was used by Clark Wissler, A. L. Kroeber, and many others. Up until about 1930 anthropologists got along quite well with Tylor's conception of culture. Probably one of the reasons why they got along with it so well is that they were working anthropologists rather than thinking anthropologists. (A great deal of good scientific work can be done without thinking, without reflective thought. One learns techniques, how to manipulate certain apparatus, and does it; this does not require thinking. As a matter of fact, a good case could be made for the proposition that thinking is really a handicap, an obstacle, in many people's professional careers.) For decades anthropologists were working: they were field anthropologists, digging up prehistoric sites, going out and salvaging disappearing cultures, recording music, languages, photographing, studying kinship systems and social organization, bringing specimens by the carload to museums, and everything was fine.

But the time came, of course, when the science became more mature, more specialized, more professionalized; and people began to think and reflect about their science, what it was and what it was all about. Then they got into trouble. Tylor's conception of culture was not expressed precisely and concisely in the form of a definition and he left a number of questions unanswered. People came to ask, "What is the nature of culture?" or "Essentially what is culture?" or "Basically what is culture?" They began to think and reflect and discuss, and the result was a great proliferation of definitions and conceptions. The point was reached where the meaning and usage of the term was so varied that it would have been possible, for instance, to get eight American and two British anthropologists together for a discussion in which "culture" would have been used in four or five senses. This made communication difficult and led to much confusion.

Let us review some of the major conceptions of culture. One very popular conception is that it exists in the mind and consists of ideas. This is quite popular and also simple-minded. This conception is based upon an obsolete anthropomorphic philosophy which still persists among some of our best anthropologists. A noteworthy example of this can be found in Walter Taylor's monograph on archaeology (1948:98,101). He says that culture consists of ideas in the mind. Such a notion is simple and explains everything. It is like saying "God did it." It "explains" culture but does not explain the ideas. The conception that culture consists of ideas is especially popular among archaeologists, perhaps because in their excavations they never come into direct contact with an idea. The correlation is so close that it makes the hypothesis plausible. What they come into contact with is projectile points, pottery, and things of that nature.

If culture consists of ideas in the mind, in whose mind are these ideas? One would think there would be no trouble here, but there has been. Anthropologists have not been able to make up their minds whether the culture which consists of ideas exists in their minds or the minds of the natives they are studying. That is an unfortunate situation. If we do not know who has the ideas, who has the culture? Cornelius Osgood (1940:25; 1951:208) was apparently the first to define culture in terms of ideas in the mind of the anthropologist, so that, for example, Crow culture existed in Lowie's mind; the Crow Indians did not have it, Lowie did.

One of the corollaries of the notion that culture consists of ideas is that there is no such thing as *material* culture. This has caused some confusion and uneasiness among some anthropologists. People had been going out collecting pottery, projectile points, baskets, bows and arrows, and so on, and putting them in museums where curators took care of them; and they thought they were dealing with culture. Then, lo and behold, they were told that these things were not culture at all. Field workers and museum curators were put in an awkward position. And the theorists were in just as bad a situation as before; for now they had to say that culture consists of ideas, the ideas cause behavior, but the behavior is not culture either: it is cultural, but not culture.

23

And an object is the product of behavior that is cultural but not culture. So we go from culture the idea to behavior which is only cultural but not culture and then finally we arrive at a product of cultural behavior. This is, to say the least, a rather clumsy and inefficient way of dealing with the concept of culture.

Another popular conception of culture is that it consists of behavior: culture is behavior. Some have added the qualification that it is learned behavior, transmitted by nongenetic means. There are innumerable definitions like this. If culture is learned behavior, the door is opened to admit subhuman species. And some anthropologists say "all right, then subhuman species do have culture." Radcliffe-Brown said that if weaver birds learn to build their nests and this learning is transmitted from one generation to another, then they have culture. Ralph Linton in *The Study of Man* (1936:78-80) and elsewhere takes the same position, i.e., there are traditions of learned behavior among subhuman species and this constitutes culture. He says we do not call it culture; we call it social heredity, but culture is merely the name that we give to human social heredity. Thus he makes no distinction in kind between the social heredity of the human species and that of nonhuman species.

The objection to the conception of culture as learned behavior is that if culture is defined in terms of learned behavior which includes subhuman species, then we must face the question, "What are we to call learned behavior which is peculiar to the human species?" (Defining culture as behavior dependent upon symboling would at least rule out the subhuman species.)

Finally, a very serious objection was noted to the learned-behavior conception of culture; namely, if culture is behavior and behavior is the subject matter of psychology, then culture belongs to the psychologists. This creates a difficult situation because it denies anthropology a subject matter; it leaves nonbiological anthropology without any subject matter. (One would think this would distress a great many anthropologists, but it did not.) As a result, Kroeber and Kluckhohn undertook to rescue nonbiological anthropology from the awful predicament of being without a subject matter. This they did in their monograph (1952) by saying, in effect, culture is not behavior but we will distinguish an abstraction of behavior from behavior itself. Then we will give the psychologists their substantial behavior and we will take the insubstantial abstraction of it for ourselves. They seem to have been quite pleased with this solution. The appearance of some subject matter was better, certainly, than not having any at all. So they emerged with this conception, which is the predominant conception of culture in American anthropology today: namely, culture is an abstraction. The idea that culture is an abstraction can be found in the works of some of the best known anthropologists and the most widely used textbooks.

Other Conceptions of Culture

We may note other conceptions of culture. One is that culture is *m* responses to *n* social signals (Zipf 1949). Geza Roheim (1943), a psychoanalytically oriented anthropologist, wrote that culture is a psychic defense mechanism. And culture has even been defined as the Rorschach of a society. What to make of these definitions or of what use they might be is obscure.

In the previous chapter we rejected and abandoned the definition of culture as behavior and the conception of culture as an abstraction. As we have seen, the reason for the latter definition, as Kroeber and Kluckhohn see it, is that behavior is the subject matter of psychology. Therefore, if culture is behavior, culture belongs to psychology, which leaves the nonbiological anthropologist empty-handed. "Since behavior is the first-hand and outright material of the science of psychology, and culture is not — being of concern only secondarily, as an influence on this material — it is natural that psychologists and psychologizing sociologists should see behavior as primary in their field, and then extend this view farther to apply to the field of culture also" (1952:155). In order to divide the territory of the social sciences between the psychologists and psychologizing sociologists, on the one hand, and the nonbiological anthropologists, on the other, Kroeber and Kluckhohn decided that culture is not behavior, but an abstraction from behavior.

In practically all discussions of culture as an abstraction, it has been assumed that those who use the word "abstraction" know what they mean by it, and furthermore, that people who read literature in which culture is defined as an abstraction will know what the word means. In other words, it has been assumed that speaker and listener alike will know what is meant by the word. These assumptions are not well founded. Nowhere, so far as we know, has any anthropologist made it clear and explicit what he meant by "abstraction." (Radcliffe-Brown discusses meanings [uses] of the term in *A Natural Science of Society* 1957:129-31.) No one has ever demanded to know what the speaker or writer meant by "abstraction." This is like dealing with things that are put in boxes and wrapped up, and then exchanging the boxes without knowing what is in them.

There has been a great confusion about what is meant by "abstraction." One of the meanings apparently was somewhat as follows: no two pottery bowls are alike, no two marriage ceremonies are exactly alike; they are numerous and varied. No two are alike, but an ideal pottery bowl, or a typical pottery bowl can be constructed by a conceptual process. So, we construct an ideal pottery bowl or ideal projectile point or ideal marriage ceremony that will represent all actual bowls, projectile points, and marriage ceremonies. This produces something like the "typical American adult male." But there is one thing Kroeber and Kluckhohn have overlooked in separating abstraction (culture) from behavior: "abstraction" applies just as much to behavior as to culture, so that these abstractions may be called *behavior* as well as culture. A marriage ceremony is behavior, and if one constructs by means of a conceptual process a typical or ideal marriage ceremony, behavior still remains behavior. It is unwarranted to say that the abstraction is not behavior but culture.

There is another possible meaning of the term abstraction. Suppose many marriage ceremonies are broken down into their component traits. Then we construct a list of these traits and see what percentage of them each marriage ceremony has. In this way we could arrive at the typical marriage ceremony, which would be an average. But this too is very much like the "typical American." This typical ceremony is a *conception,* but when it is called an abstraction instead of a conception, difficulties arise. Many anthropologists have asserted that culture, being an abstraction, is imperceptible; it is invisible, and cannot be experienced directly. This is like the inability to see the typical American who has 3.2 children because no one has 3.2 children. One cannot see this abstraction, cannot perceive it, and therefore culture cannot be perceived. And this, naturally, raises the question, "How can science have a subject matter which cannot be perceived?" There is no science that has an invisible, imperceptible, intangible subject matter; there is not and cannot be one. Then, because the "Abstractionists" have jockeyed themselves into the position that culture is imperceptible because it is an abstraction, the next logical question to be raised is, "Is culture real?" Indeed, "Does it exist?" asked Ralph Linton (1936:288,363). Radcliffe-Brown (1940:2) said culture is a word that designates no concrete reality but only an abstraction, and a very vague abstraction at that. A recent pronouncement is that of M.E. Spiro (1951:24) who says that "culture has no ontological reality." By this he evidently means that culture is not real. Thus, they have defined culture out of existence. First it is an abstraction, which is imperceptible; then it is unreal. And this, of course, leaves nonbiological anthropology with no subject matter at all. It seems fairly evident that there is and can be no science that does not have for its subject matter real things and events that exist in the external world in time and space and are observable directly or indirectly.

If one can get oneself into a situation like this by thinking, maybe one can get oneself out of it by thinking (though by a different kind of thinking). We can offer a solution to this dilemma which will give to psychology its due, and to nonbiological anthropology its due, and which will make a sharp distinction between these two. Our solution will rescue culture from the fate of annihilation and restore it to the status of concrete, observable things and events in the real world.

As mentioned in the last chapter, one of the most amazing facts in modern science is that science has had no name for one of the most important and fundamental classes of things and events that pertain to man. This is remarkable because the initial and elementary steps of science deal with classification and the naming of classes. Science begins with observation. The next step is classification and naming these classes. A large part of the glossary of science consists of names of classes of things. Yet there has been no name in the whole lexicon of science for that class of things and events that is dependent upon symboling. On the one hand this is incredible; but on the other hand it is not too surprising because, also as noted, the sciences of man are still young and undeveloped. (As a matter of fact, the concept of symboling is not widely understood. Many scientists who are concerned with man deny the significance of the concept of symbol. They are the ones who insist that the mind of man differs from the mind of subhumans only in degree.)

The process of symboling (White 1962) assumes a number of forms — thinking, feeling, acting — and we may think of the process of symboling as having products. These products are ideas, beliefs, concepts, acts, rituals, attitudes, and objects. The four main products then are ideas, attitudes, acts, and objects. They all have one thing in common: they are products of the process of symboling. They are distinguishable from all other classes of things and events, classes of things and events that are not dependent on symboling. This then is the fundamental class of things and events in the sciences of man, for which we have suggested the name "symbolate."

Now let us discuss symboling from another aspect. We begin by saying something that is probably one of the most profound and most important things that one can say in philosophy and science, even though it may appear to be silly and absurd. *A thing is just what it is.* This seems to be very difficult for people to appreciate. An act is an act. A thing is a thing. A thing is just what it is, but the *meaning* of a thing, the *significance* of a thing, in science and for us, depends not only upon its own intrinsic properties, but upon the *context* in which we consider it.

A context is an intellectual construct, a conception, an arbitrary position in which we place something for purposes of consideration and interpretation. There is no such thing as an ethical act in and of itself, or an economic act, or an erotic act, or a poetic act in itself. The acts are just what they are. But we may refer anything or any event to any context that we choose for purposes of interpretation. It might not always make sense to refer a thing or event to a certain context, but we can do it. An act is erotic when it is put in one context, but becomes ethical when you put it in another context, and economic when you put it in another. Such contexts are evident, for example, in Lewis Henry Morgan's description of Giordano's painting of Susanna and the Elders:

> . . .*Susanna. . .is partially nude ready for the bath. . .Behind the railing stands a large and powerful man in a scarlet robe with a smooth face, red cheeks and bald head, advanced in years but evidently with a keen appetite for female beauty. . .He is in the act of touching Susanna's naked shoulder with his out-stretched hand. . .Susanna is very beautiful [aesthetic], in the flower of youth, with a voluptuous form handsomely and most invitingly exposed; and . . .the Elder is. . .quite plainly a voluptuary, advancing to gratify a prurient curiosity, and excited appetite [erotic], when as an Elder and grave religious person he should have drawn back with the first glance revealing to him the true state of the case [ethical]. (White 1937:330-331)*

We need add only the commercial value of such a painting for the economic context. Anything may be referred to any context for purposes of interpretation. These contexts are not given in the external world; they are man-made. They are constructed by our minds. We do it freely and as we please. The goal and objective, of course, is to understand.

Let us return to behavior. Things and events that are dependent upon symboling are dealt with by the scientists who are concerned with man in at least two fundamentally different contexts. Insofar as they deal with things and events as symboling, the number of contexts is two and two only: the somatic context and the extrasomatic context. The terms are clumsy terms, perhaps, but serviceable for our purposes. The somatic context means dealing with something in terms of its relationship to the human organism. These things and events can also be dealt with in terms of their relationship to one another. The distinction must be made absolutely clear. On the one hand we are dealing with relationships to the human organism, and on the other hand we are not dealing with relationships to the organism at all, but relationships among symbolates themselves. Let us use the example of smoking a cigarette. This act can be referred to the somatic context, considering it in terms of its relationship to the organism. Here we deal with habit formation, satisfaction of desire, conformity to social pressure, and things of that sort. In other words, we concern ourselves with the reactions of individual organisms. In contrast, in the extrasomatic context we deal with smoking in terms of its relationship to other symbolates, such as the roles of men and women, the age dimension, smoking in certain places, what one is permitted to smoke, the pathogenic aspect of smoking, and so on. Similarly, the mother-in-law taboo can be considered in terms of the human organism; and one can also ignore the human organism completely and consider the taboo only in its relation to other customs, such as forms of marriage and descent, place of residence, etc.

That class of things and events that depend upon symboling, or which are products of symboling, considered in terms of their relationship with the human organism are in customary usage termed behavior. The scientific study of behavior is psychology, as Kroeber and Kluckhohn observed.

We also need a name for the class of things and events that depend upon symboling considered in the context of the interrelationships among the symbolates themselves. The term "culture" has traditionally been used for this purpose. (We are speaking now of actual use, not definition or conception.) The scientific study of culture then is culturology. We define culture as *that class of things and events dependent upon symboling, products of symboling, considered in an extrasomatic context* (White 1959a:234).

But should not a science have for its subject matter things and events in and of themselves: Could there not be a science whose subject matter consists of things and events considered in a certain context rather than as the things and events themselves? As a matter of fact, there are sciences that deal with things defined in terms of contexts, as, for example, parasitology, in which a variety of organisms are considered in the context of their dependence on other organisms to sustain life. Of course, in the human realm all things are significant in terms of their context. A cow is a cow, but it may be dealt with by a science of commodities, or currency.

What does our analysis of somatic and extrasomatic contexts do? First of all, it makes a sharp distinction between two fundamentally different kinds of interpretation of a specific class of phenomena. It provides us with two fundamentally different kinds of sciences. It gives and guarantees to psychology and culturology each its own sphere, its own integrity. They are not competing with each other. The question "Is the mother-in-law taboo to be explained psychologically or culturologically?" is a nonsensical question. The question, "Is the mother-in-law taboo a psychological or a culturological event?" does not make sense. It is like saying, "Is a pottery bowl an article of merchandise or an object of art?" It all depends.

There are problems that have to do with human affairs that are not psychological problems and cannot be solved psychologically. This does not belittle psychology. However, some psychologists refuse to admit that there is any problem that has to do with human beings that is not a psychological problem. It is easy to give examples of nonpsychological problems. Why do some peoples reckon descent patrilineally, others matrilineally, and others bilineally? This is not a psychological problem. Or, to take another example, why do some primitive peoples call their parallel cousins "brothers and sisters" and others call them "father and father's sister" on the paternal side and "son and mother" on the other? This also is not a psychological problem. The *problems* are not psychological, but any symbolate or combination or aggregation of symbolates may be explained or is explainable *either* psychologically or culturologically. Therefore, far from being in conflict with each other, psychologists and culturologists are really engaged in a cooperative endeavor. The culturologist cannot tell us everything we want to know about the mother-in-law taboo. We want to know how the human organism reacts to it (what does it feel like to avoid your mother-in-law, what is your conception of it) as well as how and why the custom originates and functions with respect to other customs. Nonbiological anthropology and the concept of culture are hereby rescued from disaster. We now have a real, tangible, observable subject matter for our science.

Many scientists are concerned with words. Harry Hoijer has suggested (personal communication) that instead of using the word "words" we should use "utterances." An utterance is a physical event. Let us call them "verbal utterances." Many scientists are concerned with verbal utterances. On the one hand they are dealt with in a somatic context. Here one is concerned with such things as imagination, conception, perception, habit formation, and so on. These are the things that the organism does with reference to verbal utterances. The scientific study of verbal utterances in this context is the psychology of speech. But verbal utterances also may be dealt with, not in terms of their relationship to the human organism at all, but in terms of their relationship to each other. In studying grammar, syntax, etc., both structure and process of language are dealt with as if the human race did not exist. One of the fundamental theses of the science of culture is that with reference to processes of culture change and variation, the human organism may be disregarded completely. Again, this is one of the most difficult propositions to make understood. We have already indicated (Chapter II) many people who maintain that "It is people who do it, and you can't have culture without people." There is, of course, no grammar without people either, but people are not brought into a discussion of grammatical structure.

Edward Sapir (1932:233) declared that culture cannot be realistically disconnected from the individuals who carry it. This is absolutely true, if by realistically one means in actuality. This is a fine point and one about which it is easy to be confused. Sapir deceived a considerable portion of the American Anthropological Association with this declaration! If by realistically he meant in actuality, what Sapir said is absolutely true: Culture cannot be divorced *in actuality* from people; there is no such thing as culture apart from people. But interestingly and significantly, one of the really impressive works of Edward Sapir is his monograph *Southern Paiute, a Shoshonean Language* (1930) and *there are no people in it.* It is a masterful piece of work, but there are no people in it. While it is perfectly true that culture cannot be, in actuality, disconnected from people, it *can be disconnected in logical analysis and must be for certain purposes.* And no one has done this disconnecting any better than Edward Sapir in his linguistic work.

Just as language may be studied as a distinct order of phenomena without reference to the human organism, so may culture as a whole be studied as a distinct order without reference to the human organism in the solution of certain problems. (We always exclude, of course, the questions of the origin and function of culture itself, which require a consideration of the human organism.) And language is a part of culture; the science of linguistics is a subdivision of culturology. (Incidentally, it is the most highly developed, most mature part of culturology.)

What does culture consist of? Generically it consists of ideas, attitudes, acts, and objects.

What is the locus of culture? Where does culture have its existence? Culture, where art thou? This has been a difficult question for many anthropologists to answer. Some say it exists in the mind, others say it exists in material culture so that it is on museum shelves, others say it is behavior, others say it is an abstraction from behavior, and still others say that it does not exist. Thus, people have had a hard time telling where culture has its existence. If culture consists of real, observable things and events, as it does in our conception, we ought to be able to locate it. Our answer is that culture has its existence within organisms (as ideas, sentiments, etc.), in interpersonal behavior, and in objects. These are the three loci of culture.

To avoid possible confusion, another point should be mentioned. We have said that culture has its locus within the human organism as well as among organisms in their interpersonal relations, and as well as in objects outside the human organisms. If culture may have its existence *within* human organisms, how can we talk about extrasomatic? We can because extrasomatic does not mean extraorganismic. Culture has both an intraorganismic and an extraorganismic aspect. Every culture trait has a subjective aspect. Every culture trait exists both within the human organism and outside of it. This is as true of the loathing of milk or the avoidance of a mother-in-law as it is of a stone axe. An axe is an object that has its existence outside the human organism, but it is not just a piece of stone. It is a composite of material, of conception, of attitude. It is meaningless apart from its context. Its objective aspect is its externality; its subjective aspect is its meaning and use. One might think that the avoidance of a mother-in-law is merely an attitude or a concept. But if it were only this it would be meaningless. The mother-in-law taboo is meaningless unless it is given overt expression, that is, externalized. It is given overt expression in behavior or speech or both. It exists, like the stone axe, both within the human organism (intraorganismic) and external to it (extraorganismic).

31

Culturology

The concept of culture is generally regarded as the most important and basic concept in nonbiological anthropology, but as we have already seen there has been great difficulty in achieving an adequate conception of culture.

We shall now review some of the popular definitions of culture that one finds in the literature. They represent well-established points of view.

One definition of culture has the word "characterize" in it. "Culture may be defined," says Boas (1938:159) "as the totality of mental and physical reactions and activities that characterize the behavior of the individuals composing a social group." Herskovits (1948:28) says, "When culture is closely analyzed, we find but a series of patterned reactions that characterize the behavior of individuals who constitute a given group." What Boas and Herskovits are doing is talking not about culture, but *a* culture. Let us ask this question: If culture is those traits which characterize a group, what about the traits that do not characterize it? What are they?

At this point we should discuss briefly the concept of *a* culture rather than culture in general. One speaks of Seneca culture or Iroquoian culture, or the culture of the Andean highlands. This is a perfectly legitimate form of expression, although strictly speaking there is no such thing as Seneca culture any more than there is such a thing as Republican mathematics or Baptist astronomy. This is not to say that people should not use the phrase Seneca culture. "Seneca culture" is merely a shorthand way of saying "that portion of the culture of mankind that is associated with a tribe called Seneca at a particular time and place." This is a rather long statement, so we abbreviate it by saying Seneca culture; and, of course, it is necessary to date it, because Seneca culture in 1500 is not the same as Seneca culture in 1600 and so on. *Seneca* is the name of a group of *people* that can be distinguished from other named groups of people. Because anthropologists have been much concerned with distinguishing between such things as Blackfoot culture and Arapahoe culture, or between Plains culture and Pueblo culture, they have come to define *culture in general* in terms of cultures of particular tribes or regions, and this has led to confusion. Again, to repeat the question posed above, "If culture is things which characterize a group, what about the things that do not characterize a group?" Also, is it possible to arrive at agreement as to what characterizes a tribe and what does not? It would be difficult to exaggerate the importance of distinguishing between "a culture" and "culture" in general.

Another widespread definition of culture consists of "It-takes-two-to-make-a-culture." Some anthropologists have defined culture in this way. If one person does something it is not culture. But if two do it, it is. Some insist on more than two. Linton (1945:35) says, "Any item of behavior. . .which is peculiar to a single individual in a society is not to be considered as a part of that society's culture." Durkheim (1938:lvi) says it is necessary to have several. One wonders how many is several. Wissler (1929:358) says that it is not culture unless there is a "standardized procedure established in the group," which of course raises the question, "What is standardized?" Malinowski (1941:73) says that "a cultural fact starts when an individual interest becomes transformed into public, common, and transferable systems of organized endeavor." Definitions of this sort (if, indeed, they can be called definitions) are inadequate. Some insist there must be two people involved, others that there must be several at the very least. With these criteria how can one decide when something becomes culture? It is like saying that one atom of copper is not copper, but two atoms, or several, are.

Science has to have definitions that distinguish one class of phenomena from another in terms of their *properties*, not in terms of their *number*. If there were only one whooping crane on this earth, if there were only one whooping crane in the whole cosmos, it would still be a whooping crane. Our definition of culture eliminates the difficulty of numbers very easily. Any thing or event which consists of or depends upon symboling is culture *when it is considered in an extrasomatic context.*

Another objection to the conception of culture that depends upon numbers of persons involved is that as far as human beings and human behavior and culture are concerned, there is no such thing as an individual apart from other individuals. Everything that anybody does as a human being is done in interaction with other human beings. Karl Marx (1904:268) said, "Man is in the most literal sense of the word a *zoon politikon*, not only a social animal, but an animal that can develop into an individual only in society. Production by isolated individuals outside of society. . .is as great an absurdity as the idea of the development of language without individuals living together and talking to one another."

Another conception of culture, which has caused a great deal of confusion, is that it is people, not culture, that do things. Robert S. Lynd (1939:38-39) says, "Culture does not work, move, change, but is worked, is moved, is changed. It is people who do things. . . . Culture does not enamel its fingernails or vote or believe in capitalism, but people do." This might be called the fallacy of pseudo-realism. Radcliffe-Brown (1940:10-11) wrote:

A few years ago, as a result perhaps of redefining social anthropology as the study, not of society, but culture, we were asked to abandon this kind of investigation in favor of what is now called the study of "culture contact." In place of the study of the formation of new composite societies, we are supposed to regard what is happening in Africa as a process in which an entity called African culture comes into contact with an entity called European or Western culture, and a third new entity is produced. . .which is to be described as Westernized African culture. To me this seems a fantastic reification of abstractions. European culture is an abstraction and so is the culture of an African tribe. I find it fantastic to imagine these two abstractions coming into contact and by an act of generation producing a third abstraction.

Hallowell says essentially the same thing (1945:175).

These are examples of the fallacy of pseudo-realism. Lynd and Radcliffe-Brown think they are being very realistic here. Of course, there is some reason for their writing like this; it is not *good* reason, but there is one. They have just another way of saying that you cannot have culture without people, which goes without saying, or should. (Actually, it does not go without saying; someone is always saying it.) The point is not WHO avoids his mother-in-law, WHO loathes milk, WHO writes English. The question is WHY do they do it? What has happened is that the observation of things and a scientific explanation of things have been confused. It is not a question of who does it, but why they do it and how it can be explained scientifically.

A valid and useful concept of culture has been confused and made difficult by those who speak of the reification of culture. Max Gluckman "reifies structure in precisely the way that White reifies culture," says Murdock (1951:470). William Duncan Strong (1953:392) says, "White reifies, and at times almost deifies, culture." It is considered very bad to reify culture. To reify means to make a thing of something which is not a thing. This is exactly what we have not done. It is just the opposite of what we have done. If culture were indeed an insubstantial, intangible, unreal abstraction and we treated it as a thing, then we would be guilty of reification. But the conception of culture subscribed to here, namely the Tylorian conception, is that culture consists of real things and events to start with.

And culturological explanations of these things and events help us to understand WHY. We may use numerous examples. Language is a good one. The science of linguistics is a subdivision of culturology. There are scientists who study the structure and processes of languages, make them intelligible and make generalizations about them, without reference to the human organism at all. Variation in the form of the family is another example of a phenomenon which is not explainable in terms of psychology. There are some who think that, when they have said that some people have a disposition or inclination for polyandry, they have explained polyandry.

Kinship terms provide an excellent example of the insights provided by culturological explanations. In 1939, White published an article called "A Problem in Kinship Terminology," suggesting an answer to the question, "Why is it that some kinship systems designate cross-cousins 'cousin'; other systems call them 'son' and 'daughter' on the mother's side and 'father' and 'aunt' on the father's side?" The suggested answer was that the latter form results from an emphasis on lineage. Murdock tested this hypothesis statistically in *Social Structure* (1949:125) and concluded that the evidence does indeed support this hypothesis.

Similarly, cross-cousin marriage has an effect upon kinship terminology. With cross-cousin marriage, my wife's father would be my mother's brother. Consequently, the term for mother's brother would be the same as the term for father-in-law, because my mother's brother would be my father-in-law. This type of kinship terminology is widely associated with cross-cousin marriage. Although there are tribes which have this terminology and which do not now have cross-cousin marriage, this type of terminology enables us to postulate justifiably an antecedent form of cross-cousin marriage; and this, together with other data, might enable us to reconstruct the history of their social organization.

In the field of technology we explain processes and inventions in terms of the things involved themselves. Tylor traces the evolution of the plow. On higher cultural levels we consider the evolution of the steam engine. But there are those who look with scorn upon interpretations which say, for example, that the throwing stick evolved into a boomerang. A British anthropologist, named Pitt-Rivers, in a volume of essays entitled *The Evolution of Culture and Other Essays* (1906) ridicules this notion. He says that it is absurd to say the throwing stick evolved into a boomerang. Instead, he says (p. 93) the *idea* of the throwing stick evolved into the *idea* of the boomerang. This obviously does not add anything to our understanding because there are no material culture objects without conceptions. Saying that it is the idea of the throwing stick that evolved into the idea of the boomerang explains nothing at all; it cannot tell us anything about the idea — how it originates, evolves, etc. But collecting a chronological series of forms which show transitional stages between the throwing stick and the boomerang can establish quite well and quite objectively the genealogy of the boomerang. (Incidentally, Pitt-Rivers made a noteworthy study of the evolution of firearms in western Europe, showing step by step and form by form the evolutionary process in exactly the same way that it has been shown with fossils to demonstrate the evolution of the horse.)

Ideologies also are explainable in culturological terms. There are two kinds of culturological explanation. One is that in general a certain type of ideology is associated with a certain type of technology and social system. The other deals with the interaction of concepts directly to form new combinations; it is concerned with the interaction of concepts *as such*, without reference to the brains and nervous systems of the people in which these concepts meet, interact, and form new combinations or syntheses. Darwin gives us a good example of this process in his autobiographical sketch, in which he says that he had been working on the problem of change of species and the possible origin of species for a long time but without a theory that seemed to be effective. One day, he says, he happened to read for amusement an essay on population by a man named Malthus. He encountered the idea that populations tend to increase faster than food supply. He then put this idea with other ideas, synthesizing them. "Here then I had at last got a theory with which to work," (Darwin 1888 1:68). Tylor developed a nice theory of the evolution of writing in his *Anthropology* (1881) and was able to illustrate this theory with examples from appropriate cultures and show the transition from pictographic, hieroglyphic, to alphabetic.

In this connection, something which is very illuminating and very impressive is the fact of multiple inventions or discoveries made simultaneously by people working independently of one another. Kroeber was probably the first person, at least as far as anthropological and sociological literature is concerned, to compile a list of some of these multiple, simultaneous, independent inventions and discoveries (1917). Later, William F. Ogburn published a list in his book *Social Change* (1922). He later increased this list in an article entitled "Are Inventions Inevitable?" (1922). The law of the conservation of energy, for example, was formulated four or five times by people working independently of one another in the same year. There are numerous instances of this sort (cf. White 1969:205 ff.). Newton and Leibnitz invented the calculus so near the same time that the followers of each accused the leader of the other group of plagiarism.

These facts are very interesting. How are they to be explained? We have explanations of such phenomena in terms of genes or genius. Francis Galton and William James espoused the theory that periods of great cultural development are due to genius. But this theory leaves wholly unexplained why geniuses should be abundant at certain times. In short, the genius theory provides no valid explanation at all. It explains culture change in terms of genius, but it leaves genius unexplained. It explains the known facts of culture in terms of the unknown (or unascertained) facts of biology. The reason for simultaneous inventions is perfectly simple and clear from a culturological point of view (Figs. 1 and 2). Human beings are necessary as carriers of cultural traditions; they are not necessary for an explanation of changes in these cultural traditions. This of course cannot be emphasized too greatly. If we look at a process of evolving culture and think of cultural growth, we find that when cultural evolution reaches a certain point, a certain threshold, certain syntheses of cultural traits become possible; and by becoming possible they become inevitable.

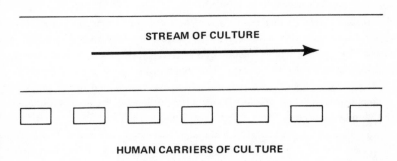

STREAM OF CULTURE

HUMAN CARRIERS OF CULTURE

Fig. 1. The stream of culture, like the flow of language, is in actuality, dependent upon its human carriers. But, this process of culture change can be discussed and made intelligible without taking the human carriers into account.

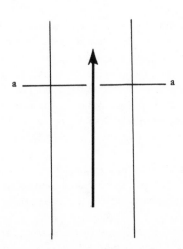

Fig. 2. This illustrates the upward flow, or development, of culture. When a certain point, a certain threshold (a,a) is reached, inventions become not only possible but inevitable.

37

Invention is a synthesis of cultural traits. Why does it rain? It rains because certain meteorological factors are present and in a certain kind of conjunction or interrelationship. It will not rain unless the conditions of humidity, atmospheric pressure, wind velocity, temperature, and perhaps other factors are present and in conjunction. If they are, then it becomes possible for it to rain, and it does rain. In that sense, rain is inevitable. If we want to use the term inevitable, this is the way we should use it. When an invention is possible, it is inevitable.

We turn now to different kinds of culturological interpretations. In what specific way does one *do* culturology? Culture is a vast body of complex and varied phenomena. These phenomena — things, acts, ideas, processes — may be dealt with in different ways. The diagram below (Fig. 3) summarizes all kinds of culturological interpretations that have been realized in the history of anthropology. The whole history of ethnological theory is embraced by this simple diagram.

	Temporal	Nontemporal
Particularizing	History	Ethnography
Generalizing	Evolution	Functionalist-Structuralist

Fig. 3. Types of culturological interpretation.

We may treat cultural phenomena in terms of their temporal or nontemporal dimensions, either with reference to time or without reference to time. Actually, of course, every cultural event takes place in time, but the flow of time might not be significant to an explanation of a phenomenon. Culture cannot be separated from its temporal context in actuality, but in logical analysis it can be. Particular points in absolute time may not be significant in a study of the process of social integration, but they would be in a history of the introduction and subsequent diffusion of the horse in aboriginal North America.

We may deal with culture in a particularizing or a generalizing way. Thus we may be interested in a particular Indian messiah at a particular time and place. Or, we may simply be interested in messiahs generally, as a sociocultural phenomena.

These two ways of interpreting cultural phenomena cross-cut each other, giving us four kinds of culturological interpretation. The temporal, generalizing interpretation gives us the evolutionist schools, concerned with a temporal sequence of forms. The nontemporal, generalizing interpretation gives us the functionalist, or, more recently, the structuralist schools. The nontemporal, particularizing concern is simply ethnography, the description of particular traits without reference to their position in absolute time.

The categories contained in Fig. 3 were derived by logical analysis from initial concepts. But this does not, of course, mean that they are merely products of the imagination, without significance for the real world. On the contrary, they correspond closely with the external world: all the schools of ethnological theory are neatly accommodated by our diagram (see the diagram in White 1968). We may note also that this diagram, and the types of interpretation which it implies, are applicable to inanimate and biological, as well as to culturological, phenomena.

Culture as System

We perhaps have not said quite enough about the distinction between psychological and culturological interpretations of phenomena associated with the human species. We might, therefore, review rather rapidly some examples which will further illustrate the differences (see also "Culturological vs. Psychological Interpretations of Human Behavior" in White 1969).

Some psychologists believe that anything pertaining to man as a human being, any problem, is a psychological problem. It is perfectly true that any phenomena peculiar to the human species, i.e., dependent upon symboling, are a part of the proper subject matter of psychology. But raw phenomena, raw data, are one thing; scientific problems are something else. One can formulate many problems that have to do simply with people speaking to each other: the sheer mechanics of the muscles that are involved, the organs of speech, the thermodynamics aspect of the energy required, the production of waves in the atmosphere, and so on. These are purely physical problems. A problem is the formulation of a question asked about a certain class of phenomena, and many different kinds of questions can be asked about the same kind of phenomena. In the case of vocal, verbal communication between persons, we can distinguish physical, physiological, neurological, psychological, and culturological problems. The failure to distinguish between raw phenomena on the one hand and scientific problems on the other has led some psychologists to believe that *all* problems having to do with human beings belong properly to psychology. This is simply not true.

Psychologists have attempted, for example, to account for the origin of incest taboos, but are unable to produce a satisfactory theory. Nor can their theories throw light upon the variations of this taboo as we find it in various cultures. The problem of the origin of incest taboos is not a psychological problem, but a culturological problem. An attempt has been made to set forth a culturological solution to this problem (White 1948). Very briefly, the gist of the culturological explanation of the origin of incest taboos is this: given symboling and articulate speech, cooperation and mutual aid within families becomes possible, and cooperative endeavor has a positive biological survival value. This cooperation is then extended from *within* families to *among* families or between families. The incest taboo was a way of prohibiting intra-familial marriage in order to compel people to marry into other families and thus establish cooperative ties, form mutual aid groups, and make life more secure.

War is another phenomenon that has often been explained psychologically: war is a kind of activity that men engage in because of their inborn, innate tendencies. It is very interesting to note that two of our best-known anthropologists have contributed to this psychological theory of war. Ralph Linton (1936:461) said that the Plains Indians were not fighting over food or land; they were just fighting for fun. Ruth Benedict (1942:763) says that men just like war. William James discourses in "The Moral Equivalent of War" upon the love of glory and the pugnacious instinct that has been bred into the bones and marrow of men for years, and that is what causes war. More recently we have the frustration and aggression theory. A number of psychologists since William James have suggested that we engage in great international athletic contests, as a way to world peace.

The trouble with theories of this sort is that they do not, and cannot, explain who fights whom, when, and where. Furthermore, the alleged psychological causes are not observed directly; they are merely inferred. No hypothesis or postulate is of much value if it does not rest upon observed facts. The only way we know that people are frustrated is because there is a war. It is assumed that they could not have gone to war for any reason other than frustration. A discussion of war in terms of degrees of cultural development, such as we find in Tylor (1881:225), i.e., in terms of such activities as exploiting the resources of nature, gives us a much more realistic and intelligible explanation of war than all the psychological explanations.

Warfare is virtually unknown among many peoples. Everywhere, however, where culture outgrows the tribal stage, and sometimes before then, war is a natural phenomenon, a natural form of interaction between tribes or nations. What they are fighting for becomes quite plain in many instances. They are fighting for the resources of nature, a means of life. This was true of the Plains Indians; they were not fighting "just for fun," although it is true that they did make a game of warfare, of killing. But they were fighting for their territories and for food resources. Warfare increased as the White man drove eastern tribes out into the Plains, intensifying competition. The struggle for existence became even more intense. They were fighting to live. (See Newcomb 1950).

In the preceding chapter we discussed inventions as syntheses of already existing cultural elements. A culturological definition of a genius or great inventor is that he is simply a person in whose nervous system this synthesis of cultural elements has taken place (cf. White, 1969:ch. VIII). The synthesis occurs because this particular nervous system is at the right place at the right time. The culturologist knows as well as anyone else that no two people are alike; the assumption that people differ in their native abilities seems to be very well supported in spite of the fact that many of these abilities cannot be measured accurately. Culturologists accept these facts readily. There seems to be good reason to believe that a perfectly average mind that is in the right place at the right time can achieve much more from the standpoint of cultural progress than an exceedingly able one that is not in the right place at the right time. The actual achievement is made much more intelligible in terms of the operation of cultural forces and their influence upon the nervous system, and their synthesis within it, than by our inferential estimates of innate ability.

What we have said here about inventions and great men applies equally well to individuals in the fine arts. Beethoven is explainable and made more intelligible in terms of a culturological account of the evolution of music in the Western world and by showing how this musical tradition influenced him, than he is by mere consideration of his nerves and sense organs. We assume that Beethoven had superior neural equipment because he is identified with a very high degree of development of a particular musical tradition. In the realm of politics, history, and war, we find the greatest, most extravagant and realistic expression of the theory of the "Great Man." The extent of this doctrine of great-manism is enormous. It is an expression of old anthropomorphic and anthropocentric ways of looking at things, and of course journalism exploits it tremendously. *Time* magazine once wrote in its editorial that it uses this interpretation because this is what its readers want, and because it makes events more intelligible to them by saying that Stalin did this, Stalin wanted that, etc. Since certain individuals are the heads of government or leaders of armies, and have been involved in great events, therefore these individuals are great men: they were the causes, the designers and "doers" of these events.

This is a very plausible theory, but it has virtually nothing to commend it as far as science is concerned. Governments have to have heads; armies have to have generals. Even if all men were absolutely equal in ability, the only way an army could be effective would be to have someone at the head of it. It is a function of social organization, of social structure. If a great man is great because he is associated with a successful achievement, then he is not great if he fails; great generals are the ones on the winning side.

We come now to a question which is difficult to discuss realistically and effectively: "Is it not possible that the great man, that is, the man in a high position in politics, government, or war, leaves his imprint upon the course of historical events, that he affects the course of history by virtue of his own abilities?" Or, in other words, "Would not the course of history have been different if someone else had been in that place?" The answer to that question is yes. This is the only thing that can be said in support of the theory that individuals may be significant in social and cultural events (i.e., individuals as such). The individual is not significant in evolution but he may be in history. Of course men like Lincoln, Lenin, and Hitler affect the course of history; nonentities like John Wilkes Booth may have, and have had, a profound effect. It is perfectly true that the individual's characteristics and the psychological abilities of anyone are significant whether they are marked or mediocre. But any kind of an individual can have these consequences: it does not even have to be a human being. It could be a dog, a rabbit, a meteorite ("For want of a nail. . ."). The theory of the great man in history boils down really to an admission of the fact that anything can do it. To reiterate, the individual is not significant in evolution, but may be in history.

Let us conclude our discussion of psychology and culturology thus: the subject matter of human psychology and culturology is one and the same class of phenomena, which is the reason why there can be conflicts between them. If they did not have something in common, they would have nothing to fight over. However, it does not follow that there is no difference between a psychological *problem* and a culturological one merely because these sciences deal with the same subject matter. Although they deal with the same phenomena, they deal with them in fundamentally different contexts, with different problems and different solutions. For a complete knowledge and understanding of *any* phenomenon dependent upon symboling, *both psychology and culturology are necessary.* Whereas the culturologist would explain why and how the polygynous family came to be, the psychologist would tell us how the human organism responds to this institution and reacts within it.

Let us now turn to the concept of a cultural system. The sociologist has for generations been familiar with the concept of society as a system. Herbert Spencer not only gave us the concept of society but likened it to the concept of system in biology, which of course is organism. In *The Study of Sociology* he has a chapter called "Society is an Organism."

What is a system? A system is an organization of phenomena so interrelated that the relation of part to part is determined by the relation of part to whole. In a tribe the relationship of individual to individual is determined by the relationship of the individual to the whole. This is what a system is. We may consider culture as a distinct order of phenomena, and the possibility and desirability of doing this has been expressed and demonstrated by culturologists for generations. Robert H. Lowie has given explicit expression to this view (e.g., 1917:1936). If culture can be considered as a distinct order of phenomena, studied, interpreted and explained without reference to human organisms insofar as its variations are concerned, how are we to think of culture as organized into systems? This question can be answered by observing cultural phenomena, and noting if they do — or do not — conform to our conception and definition of system. Observations make it evident that culture does constitute a system, i.e., it is organized systematically. We may consider the culture of mankind as a whole or we may consider some portion of this totality. The culturologist constructs models, either of the culture of mankind as a whole or of a particular culture. These are ideal structures as all models are. Their justification consists of their utility in providing us with insight and understanding of the real world.

Take, for example, the model of a cultural system. It does not make any difference here whether it is the culture of mankind as a whole or any portion thereof. The model of *a* culture will be the same, for certain purposes at any rate, as the model of the culture of mankind as a whole. A cultural system as we would model-build it consists of three or four categories of cultural phenomena, depending upon what one wants to do with it. The fact that there could be three or four different categories indicates the arbitrariness and artificialness of the model being built. The external world does not vary, but models may. Cultural models are composed of technological, sociological, and ideological elements. Attitudes or sentiments may be included as a fourth category, if desired. Whether or not these are included depends upon the purpose of the model.

Old Herbert Spencer used to talk about the "morphology and physiology" of society. If societies are organisms, why not talk about their morphology and physiology? Functionalists like Malinowski were concerned with the function, or physiology, of culture; but they also talked about the anatomy and skeleton of culture. The early functionalists, whose emphasis then was on process or physiology, also had "anatomy" in their glossary. As noted before, the successors of the early functionalists now call themselves structuralists; the emphasis has shifted from physiology to anatomy. We have here the recognition of both structure and processes of a cultural system.

This leads us to a theory that is probably the most realistic and fundamental conception we have of cultural systems. It enables us to do more and better work, to solve more problems, than any other conception of cultural systems. Namely, the fundamental component of any cultural system is its technological apparatus; upon this foundation of technology, social systems rest; and above both, as part of the superstructure, are ideologies. The technological component of cultural systems is fundamental because it is at this point that the life-sustaining adjustment between man as an animal and the surface of the earth is effected. This conception of a cultural system is the exact opposite of one which is, perhaps, most popular which says that the basic and fundamental thing in cultural systems is ideas. One cannot lecture on cultural systems without having someone speak up and say that it is not technology at all, it is ideas. But man cannot subsist on ideas; he has to have food. He must exploit the resources of nature. And the direct and immediate ways and means of exploiting the resources of nature, without which life and culture are not possible, are technological.

Social systems rest upon technology as a foundation. As a matter of fact, a realistic and justifiable way of looking at institutions is as follows: Institutions are the ways in which a group of human animals use technological means in order (1) to obtain food, which is the primary need of life, and (2) to protect themselves from their enemies, which is secondary. What *is* social organization except the ways in which peoples use their technology to get food and protect themselves? The way that question is asked would suggest that there is nothing else in social organization except food-getting and protection. There are other things, of course. But these other things are secondary and are in turn dependent upon the way in which food is obtained and protection provided. Social systems are functions of technological systems; they are determined by technological systems. Technological systems are the independent variables, social systems the dependent variables. The social organization of a hunting and gathering tribe is not, cannot, and could not be the same as the social organization of a sedentary, agricultural tribe. The social organization of the highly industrialized United States of 1970 could not be the same as the social organization of rural, agricultural United States in 1783.

Ideologies or philosophies are also functions of technology. A culture in which the highest level of technological development is represented by a stone axe, and another one in which the highest technological development is a plow, and still another in which it is a spectroscope or a digital computer, are ideologically different. Those items of technology are indicative of, and producers of, different philosophies. Ideologies are a function of technology. Ideologies originate within technological processes, but they are passed through social systems and are influenced by them before they find overt expression in philosophy. Therefore, it is quite possible to have cultural systems with similar and comparable technologies but with different ideologies. The United States and Russia, for example, have similar technologies but their ideologies are different because they are refracted by different political and economic systems.

History of the Theory of Cultural Evolution

The theory of evolution is applicable to culture from three standpoints: first, to the culture of mankind as a whole; second, to the culture of any distinguishable group of people and any distinguishable area (distinguishable in the sense that significant differences among them can be observed); and, third, to subsystems within a cultural system as a whole, such as, for example, social organization, writing, mathematics, etc. We cannot apply the concept of evolution to anything that cannot properly be considered a system. Thus, we cannot talk about the evolution of windows because they cannot be considered as systems in any meaningful sense. Nor can we discuss the evolution of feet (of insects, birds, mammals, etc.) because they are not systems in themselves but merely parts of systems. Likewise, in the realm of culture we cannot trace the course of the evolution of the family because families are integral parts of social systems (although a particular kind of family in its own cultural matrix may be considered as a system in this limited sense; it took anthropology a long time to discover these important facts). We must also be careful about talking about the evolution of *a* culture, whether it be of a particular tribe or a particular region, because its inherent evolutionist process may be profoundly affected by diffusion from the outside. But, with regard to subsystems within the realm of culture, we may meaningfully discuss the evolution of social organization (the emergence of clan organization, etc.), of writing as a whole, of mediums of exchange in general to coined money in particular, etc.

The theory of cultural evolution has been one of the most important questions in nonbiological anthropology since Darwin. There is a vast literature on the subject. The concept of evolution in cultural anthropology has had a rather bizarre history. It is incredible (so incredible that it is difficult to explain to non-anthropologists) that a discipline calling itself a science could have repudiated and rejected one of the most basic, fundamental, and fruitful theories in the whole history of science. But this is what cultural anthropology, especially in the United States, did. This action on the part of cultural anthropology was reactionary, that is, in direct and deliberate opposition to a trend which by consensus is progressive. It was anti-progressive. Within this century, only orthodox theology and cultural anthropology have opposed the theory of evolution.

The first school of ethnological theory was evolutionist. Why was it evolutionist rather than historical or functionalist? The answer seems to be because scientific theory was taking the place of theological theory. Theological theory held that mankind was created and culture was instituted by the Creator. When the theological interpretation was abandoned, any new theory that could take its place had to do what theology had previously done, namely, to show how man and culture had originated and how culture had developed. The only scientific theory that could do this was an evolutionary theory. Culture history could not do this because (1) the facts necessary for history were not available, and (2) because a history of culture can reveal what happened, when it happened, and where it happened; but it can not show *why* it happened. This the evolutionary theory can do. This is why the first of the scientific ethnological theories was evolutionary.

Works on cultural evolution appeared shortly after the publication of *The Origin of Species* in 1859. The scientific and intellectual world became not only receptive to evolutionary theory but very enthusiastic about it. For a number of decades the theory of evolution in cultural anthropology continued to be developed and enjoyed a great vogue. The great pioneers in cultural evolutionism were: (1) Herbert Spencer, primarily in his *Principles of Sociology.* He was not really a culturologist, although it was he who invented the term "superorganic" which was subsequently used by Kroeber as a title for one of his first and most significant contributions to culturology (1917); (2) E. B. Tylor, among whose contributions are *Primitive Culture* (1871) and *Anthropology* (1881); and (3) Lewis H. Morgan, author of *Ancient Society* (1877).

During the 1880s and especially in the 1890s a reaction against cultural evolutionism began in Germany and the United States. It grew and developed until the whole theory of the evolution of culture was rejected, repudiated, scoffed at, and ridiculed. In 1918, one of our prominent anthropologists, Berthold Laufer, favorably reviewed (p. 90) a book by Robert H. Lowie in which Lowie discussed the theory of cultural evolution. Laufer said, "The theory of cultural evolution is in my mind the most inane, sterile, and pernicious theory in the whole history of science." This expressed the attitude of American anthropologists toward the theory for a very long time. The leader of the antievolutionist movement in the United States was Franz Boas, who exerted great influence upon American anthropologists and anthropology for several decades.

In Europe, criticism of evolutionism began with Ratzel, an anthropogeographer. But it did not become very significant until it was taken over by a

47

German anthropologist named Fritz Graebner and some of his co-workers. With the decline of Graebner's health and influence, the criticism of evolutionism was taken over by Father Wilhelm Schmidt and his co-worker Father Wilhelm Koppers. It then became a vigorous, articulate, and indefatigable antievolutionist movement.

Antievolutionism made little headway in England. England was the stronghold of cultural evolutionism for a long time. The first exception occurred about 1910 or 1911 when W. H. R. Rivers became "converted" to diffusionism. (The word "convert" implies, of course, that it is an article of faith. There has been a great deal of sectarianism in anthropology; much of cultural anthropology has been organized into sects with articles of faith, with prophets and disciples. See, for example, White 1966.) Rivers's conversion to diffusionism opened a breach in the wall of evolution, so to speak, in England. Another diffusionist school, the heliolithic school of Elliot Smith and W. J. Perry, had relatively little influence upon science.

In addition, as a consequence of the Torres Straits expedition in 1898, in which English anthropologists for the first time did systematic field work (in Melanesia), the functionalist school emerged. Functionalism is a conception, or theory, that is most congenial to field work, because the field worker sees cultural systems in action and is confronted by their structures and processes. So functionalism started in England very much as a consequence of the Torres Straits expedition. The functionalist school became the predominating school in Britain. When referring to evolutionism, the functionalists spoke disparagingly or scoffed at it, but they did not really attack it often. They were simply not interested in it.

There are two kinds of reasons for opposition to the evolutionist school (school rather than theory): scientific and nonscientific. Scientific criticism of the evolutionist school consisted of arguing that cultural similarities in noncontiguous areas must be (and indeed, in many instances they were) due to diffusion and not to independent parallel development resulting from the psychic unit of mankind. One of the postulates of the evolutionist school was that man's mind everywhere is basically the same, that everywhere he has the same needs, and that therefore, by and large, the cultures of mankind would develop along the same lines, with any differences being due to local differences in habitat or circumstances. This meant that cultural similarities in noncontiguous areas were due to the inherent nature of man. Some evolutionists pushed this theory as far as it would go, and farther than it could be substantiated. One of the most extreme of the evolutionists was the most distinguished anthropologist in the United States in the 1890s, Daniel Garrison Brinton (1900). He has been almost forgotten by subsequent generations. He was an extremist of the evolutionist school, and said a number of things that could not be substantiated. He argued, for example, that the similarities between the mythologies of the Iroquoian tribes and the neighboring Algonkian tribes were not due to diffusion, but to psychic unity; that the cultures of the New World and the Old World were entirely independent; that the cultures of the Andean highlands and Mexico grew up wholly independently.

The first person to criticize this point of view effectively was Ratzel, who collected a great deal of evidence with regard to bows in Africa and with fact and reason provided a convincing argument for the diffusion of bows from one region to another. Boas did likewise with regard to mythology on the Northwest Coast.

Lowie said that one of the most fundamental questions in ethnological theory is the question of diffusion versus independent development. And it was in this context that evolutionist theory was scientifically criticized and opposed. However, it was shown, for example, that the similarities between the pyramids of Mexico and those of Egypt are superficial. Their construction is different. In Mexico, they are mounds of earth faced with stone; in Egypt they are completely of stone. In Mexico they are solid; in Egypt they have chambers within them. The function of pyramids in Egypt was to enclose tombs of the royalty; in Mexico they were substructures for temples. Structurally and functionally, therefore, they were different. So the argument for diffusion in this case was greatly weakened, if not destroyed entirely. The same was true with regard to some other specific issues. The question of diffusion versus independent development is one of fact, not of theory. In other words, decisions as to whether cultural similarities in noncontiguous areas are due to diffusion or to independent development can be made only upon the basis of facts, plus, of course, reason. The similarities may be due to one process in one case and the other process in another. It is not an all-or-none proposition.

We turn now to the nonscientific opposition to the theory of evolution in cultural anthropology. We shall defer a brief attempt at an explanation for this nonscientific opposition until after we have reviewed some of the ways in which arguments against cultural evolution were phrased. We shall limit the discussion to cultural anthropology and not include opposition outside of anthropology, although a great deal of opposition came from other sources.

There were many arguments against cultural evolutionism. Boas and his students spent much time and effort in an attempt to destroy cultural evolutionism. A Jesuit Priest named Father Joseph J. Williams, writing about Boas in a Jesuit journal (*Thought* 1936), remarks that Boas and his students fought the theory of evolution in culture indefatigably for over twenty-five years. Goldenweiser, who has been called the most philosophical of Boas's students, wrote several antievolutionism articles over a period of twenty-five years (1914-1937). Lowie's *Primitive Society,* which is probably his most important and significant work, is to a great extent an attack upon cultural evolutionism and is recognized as such by its reviewers. Sapir, Benedict, Herskovits, and Kroeber have paid lip service to antievolutionism, if not more.

Let us review some of the arguments that have been presented. These arguments were developed, made explicit, and taught as articles of faith, and we do not know how many generations of graduate students have learned these and passed them on. (This is what culture does to people, of course. Education is a process of transmitting culture from one generation to another.)

One argument was that the theory of evolution was borrowed from biology and applied to culture. This was done, it was said, because of the prestige and success of Darwinism in biology. Sapir said that ethnologists wanted to ape biologists. This idea has had a great vogue and many people have subscribed to it. As a matter of fact, it is repeated by Claude Lévi-Straus, who is not a member of the Boas school, in an article as recent as 1949 (p. 365).

What is wrong with this criticism? The main thing wrong is that it is not true. The theory of cultural evolution antedated Darwin considerably. There were many exponents of the theory of cultural evolution before Darwin: Lucretius, Ibn Kaldun, Bossuet, Hume, Condorcet, Immanuel Kant, von Herder, Bachofen, Comte, and Letourneau, among others. Interestingly enough, some evolutionists were willing to argue that *culture* evolved but they were not willing to accept the theory of biological evolution because they did not think it could be sufficiently supported by fact. Furthermore, neither Spencer, Tylor, nor Morgan borrowed the concept of evolution from biology. Spencer antedated Darwin. In 1852, Spencer set forth the theory of evolution in comprehensive form in an essay called "The Development Hypothesis," a theory that was equally applicable to biological phenomena and to superorganic phenomena. In the preface to the second edition of *Primitive Culture* Tylor explains why no reference was made to Darwin — because his work had developed quite independently of Darwin. Tylor was a mature scholar before the publication of *The Origin of Species.* And Morgan's work grew out of his own studies of the Iroquois and kinship systems. He did not even become acquainted with Darwin's book until after his own theory of evolution had developed.

The preceding argument of the antievolutionists is invalid because (1) the theory of cultural evolution existed *prior* to Darwin; (2) the cultural evolutionists did not borrow from Darwin; and (3) the theory of evolution *is*, in fact, applicable to cultural phenomena as well as to biological phenomena. (The notion that the theory of evolution is applicable only to biological phenomena is a prejudice that still persists.) Here, then, is one of the antievolutionist arguments. It has been very effective; it was imparted from one generation to another, was written in textbooks, and became established dogma for decades.

50

Another argument that also was very effective, in the sense that it succeeded in extirpating the theory of cultural evolution from anthropological literature, was the argument that evolutionism in cultural phenomena was unilinear, and unilinear was bad, so therefore evolutionism was bad. We must try to understand what unilinear evolution means, says Boas (1938:178). It means, he says, that every society must pass through the same stages of development. This conception was attributed to the so-called classical evolutionists: Spencer, Tylor, and Morgan.

What is wrong with this argument? Again, the main thing that is wrong is that it is not true. No evolutionist ever said this. How can we explain why this argument was accepted? How is it possible, in general, for errors to persist? One of the reasons that this particular error could persist is that the people to whom this doctrine was taught did not read the evolutionists, and many of those who taught it had not read them either. Paul Radin, in a retrospective article about Boas (1939:303), remarks that the writings of Morgan were anathema to Boas and his students and "remained unread." None of the evolutionists ever said that every *society* has to pass through certain stages. What they did say was that *culture,* or portions thereof, passed through stages of development. No evolutionist, for example, ever said that each people had to pass through a stage of hieroglyphic writing before they could adopt alphabetic writing. What Tylor said was that writing evolved in a series of stages beginning with picture writing, passing through hieroglyphic writing to alphabetic writing; that is, picture writing could not leap to alphabetic writing but an intermediate stage of hieroglyphic writing was an essential part of the process. And it is inconceivable that Morgan, living side by side with Iroquois people, seeing their children going to school, learning the alphabet directly without passing through a stage of hieroglyphic writing, could have thought such a thing!

The unilinear argument became very effective when applied to the cultures of Africa. In Africa, so the antievolutionists said, various peoples passed directly from the stone age to the iron age; and since it was asserted that the evolutionists had said that *all peoples* had to pass through the stages of chipped stone, polished stone, copper, bronze, and iron, and African tribes had not done this, therefore, the theory of evolution collapses. This argument is also invalid. In the first place, the evolutionists (Morgan and Tylor) knew the facts of African culture history as well as the antievolutionists did; they knew that the bronze age had been "skipped." Incidentally, Tylor said there is still a question as to which was worked first, copper or iron (1881:219). So, he did not even think that in the art of metallurgy certain materials had to be worked first. (However, the evolutionists, thanks to the investigations of Danish archaeologists, did establish a stone, bronze, iron sequence.) The first criticism, then, is that the evolutionists knew the African sequence. In addition, the argument is irrelevant because the evolutionists never said that *peoples* had to go through these stages. They said that by and large this is the sequence of stages in technology, which is a valid statement.

The unilinear argument leads to a more generalized criticism of evolutionism which we may call "diffusion versus evolutionism." This argument has been tremendously effective. It runs as follows: One cannot talk about the evolution of Seneca culture, or Plains culture, because the process of development would be so disturbed by diffusion that evolution would be rendered impossible. We may illustrate this thesis with the following diagram (Fig. 4):

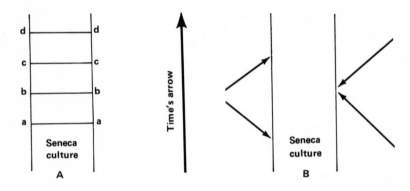

Fig. 4. Evolutionism negated by diffusion.

Time is flowing upward as indicated by the arrow. In A, we have a hypothetical situation: a culture in isolation, wholly uninfluenced by other cultures. It may, therefore, develop freely, passing through stages a, b, c, and d in order. But, in actuality, tribes and cultures are not isolated, i.e., wholly uninfluenced from the outside. On the contrary, they are besieged with cultural influences, operating by means of diffusion, as shown in B. These diffusionist influences so disturb the course of development that regular stages of development cannot be detected. Therefore, theories of cultural evolution are invalid.

But this argument has a serious defect. Again, no evolutionist said that each culture (which in effect means each people) must pass through a certain series of stages of development. What they said was that culture as a whole, or certain distinguishable portions thereof, such as writing, had to pass through certain stages. And this sequence of stages is not upset by diffusion.

Still another argument against evolutionism which has been very effective is one that the president of the American Anthropological Association used in a session of the Association not very long ago. This is the "Australian aborigines" argument, which runs as follows: Australian tribes have a very highly developed social system with a very primitive technological system. This is incompatible with the evolutionist theory that there is a close and necessary correlation between social system and technology. This has been a very persuasive argument. What may have been meant by "highly developed" or "complex" was that it was difficult for some anthropologists to understand the kinship system. Gladys Reichard said (1938:412-13) that some teachers are just simply appalled by the kinship system of the Arunta, meaning, perhaps, that they did not understand it. But the Arunta did not have any trouble with it, and quite a number of anthropologists are able to understand it and transmit some understanding of it to others. There is no question at all about the crudeness of the technology of the Australian cultures. And on no legitimate grounds can the social systems of the aborigines be called highly developed. (Complexity does not necessarily mean highly developed. As a matter of fact, what is more complex than a single living cell?) The social organization of Australian aborigines has two fundamental units: the local territory group and the family. The kinship system of the Arunta, which, compared to ours might be called complex, is based upon the family and a simple rule of marriage: marriage to mother's mother's brother's daughter, or in other words, one's second cross-cousin. There is no tribal organization. Except within the family, there is no division of labor. Their social organization, thus, is extremely simple, primitive. Even prehuman primates have the local territory group and the family (cf. White 1949:371-72).

Another criticism of evolutionism was that it was ethnocentric. The critics of evolutionism said that what the evolutionists did was to arrange all cultures into a series dependent upon similarities and differences with our own culture. Our (western European) culture was put at the top, the cultures that were most different from ours put at the bottom, and the others arranged in a series according to their similarities and differences with respect to our culture. This was said to be unwarranted because it was a subjective evaluation (arbitrary, ethnocentric, unscientific) and that by other criteria cultures would be arranged in a different way. In Goldenweiser's *Early Civilization* ("the first real textbook on anthropology" in America, Mead and Bunzel 1960:508) he advances an argument similar to the more general one about putting our culture at the top. He says that the five cultures he had described could be arranged in any way you choose: if you take ingenuity and skill, technology and adjustment to habitat, the Eskimos would be at the top. If you take political organization, the Iroquois are at the top. He says it all depends upon how the criteria are selected (p. 125); the judgments are arbitrary and subjective and therefore nonscientific.

This argument has been a dogma in at least part of the Boas school. It is implicit in the works of Boas and is explicit in Margaret Mead, Ruth Benedict, and Lowie: one cannot evaluate cultures; one culture is just as good as another, which of course denies or refutes evolutionist theory because evolutionist theory maintains that cultures proceed from the simple to the complex, from the primitive to the highly developed.

As a matter of fact, placing Western culture at the top can be justified by the application of objective standards of measurement. All means of measurement are arbitrary. Standards and criteria vary. There are, of course, subjective criteria and standards, and these cannot be used by science. But the fact that there are subjective criteria does not mean that there are no meaningful and valid objective criteria. The function of culture is to make life secure for the human species by the exercise of control over the habitat and forces of nature. Of course one could say, for example, "Well, my criterion of culture is, who is happy?"; but that is nonsense. It is not science, and science is what we are concerned with.

From a scientific standpoint, there are objective criteria by means of which cultures can be evaluated and thereby arranged in series from simple to complex, from primitive to civilized. The criterion is the exercise of control over the resources and forces of nature by technological means. The amount of food per unit of human labor is a relationship that can be measured objectively and expressed quantitatively, mathematically. Control over disease is an objective index. Average length of life can be measured. There are many other specific and particular measurements. The productivity of culture varies. It varies as the technology varies, other things being constant. Cultures can be evaluated by objective standards. Differences are measurable. Using such measurements, placing our culture at the top becomes legitimate, because our culture has the greatest control over the resources and forces of nature. The assertion that one cannot grade cultures flies in the face of common sense and science. To say, for example, that it is unwarranted to assert that the culture of the Aztecs was not more highly developed than that of the Indians of Tierra del Fuego does not make sense. To say that the culture of the United States in 1783 was neither higher nor lower than the culture of the United States in 1963 does not make sense, except, perhaps, to some who were trained in the Boasian tradition.

Another popular argument, and one of the weakest arguments of all (all arguments that are arguments of faith and not of fact and reason are weak) was that it was field work that destroyed evolutionist theory. The Boas school made a fetish of field work. They maintained that they were inductive and empirical and, by contrast, by assertion and implication, the cultural evolutionists were armchair philosophers (although Sapir called them "closet philosophers," 1920:377). Evolutionists just spun theories out of their heads.

As a matter of fact, Morgan, who was most often called the armchair philosopher, was the great pioneer of field work in ethnology. Morgan made an exhaustive study of the Iroquoian tribes through field work and published a comprehensive synopsis of Iroquoian culture years before Franz Boas was born. He did thorough, intensive field work. In addition, at no point have the antievolutionists shown how field work has destroyed evolutionist theory; they have merely made the assertion. Nor have they provided any good reason why field work should negate evolutionist theory. Theory is based on facts, but the same facts can support more than one theory. The association of human remains with extinct animals in Europe was explained by two quite different theories. It was not the discovery of new facts that made Christian theological anthropology obsolete, but a new theory did. In other words, it was armchair thinking. It would take only one instance of human remains found in association with extinct animals to "knock Christian theological theory of the creation into a cocked hat." There were dozens of such discoveries known in Europe for at least a century and a half before Darwin. It was not new facts that provided the theory of Darwinism, it was thinking; it was armchair philosophizing. One of the reasons why the Boas group has extolled induction and empiricism is probably that Franz Boas did not exemplify reflective thought.

There is an instance in which a specific evolutionist theory was rendered invalid by the discovery of facts, and it applies not to evolutionists in general, but to Morgan in particular. With regard to the origin of human social organization, Tylor and Morgan were at opposite poles. Morgan postulated that mankind began with a condition of promiscuity; Tylor maintained that man had the family from the beginning. Morgan's theory (greatly simplified) of primordial promiscuity, followed by a stage of polygamy and finally monogamy, is incompatible with ethnographic facts (facts which were, incidentally, unknown to Morgan). The facts are that it is precisely among the most primitive peoples of the world that we find the highest coefficient of monogamy; polygamy flourishes on intermediate levels. The facts are, therefore, almost the opposite of what Morgan predicted: monogamy on the earliest level, not on the last. Here, then, is one instance in which ethnographic investigation brought forth evidence which negated, not evolutionist theory in general (it is quite compatible with Tylor's evolutionary theory) but Morgan's in particular.

Morgan's whole theory of the evolution of the family is obsolete and has been for some time. Radcliffe-Brown and Lowie both said that Morgan held this theory because he was a mid-Victorian to whom monogamy was the highest form of development, and therefore primitive man must have been at the opposite extreme. That is misrepresentation. Morgan developed his theory of the evolution of the family as a consequence of an attempt to explain the different systems of kinship terminology that he had discovered and which he had collected by field work. His theory grew directly out of his field work. The idea that field work destroyed evolutionist theory is weak and unsupported. (Incidentally, almost all the arguments against evolution have been mere assertions. *Not a single argument ever quotes a specific evolutionist.* What the evolutionists say is asserted, but not quoted, and one is never encouraged to "go and read them and see for yourself.")

As for nonscientific attacks on cultural evolutionism, we may note that although Darwinism triumphed for a time, so old, strong and well-entrenched were nonscientific and nonevolutionist theories everywhere (in theology, in institutions, in most philosophies) that antievolutionism was not extinguished by Darwinism. This we know from the Scopes trial as well as from many other events. And antievolutionism is not dead yet, by any means, in the schools or outside of them, or in anthropology or outside of it. Much of the prescientific, antievolutionist tradition that existed before Darwin still persists. Scientific and evolutionist theories have not yet acquired sufficient strength, weight, and momentum to extinguish the prescientific theories.

Also, Morgan's theory of the evolution of culture in general and of property in particular was incompatible with our capitalist ideology. Furthermore, his *Ancient Society* was adopted by Karl Marx and became a Marxist classic. As a consequence, his theory of cultural evolution was rejected by capitalist, democratic ideology. Here we have streams and currents in the intellectual traditions of the Western world which have ages, time dimensions, weights, magnitudes, and directions. These traditions are competing with one another. And, as we have seen, for a long period of time the prescientific, antievolutionist theories predominated.

How Culture Evolved

In the development of scientific thought, the concept of energy has emerged as the most universal and fundamental of all concepts. Everything in the cosmos can be described in terms of energy, whether it be galaxies, solar systems, biological systems, nonhuman social systems, or sociocultural systems. Thinking about energy found expression in laws of thermodynamics, of which there are three. The first law of thermodynamics says in effect that the total amount of energy in the cosmos is a constant. The second law of thermodynamics says in effect that the cosmos is moving in the direction of greater disorder and wider diffusion of energy, that it is breaking down structurally and running down dynamically, and that the chronological and logical end of this process, if there be an end, is chaos. It is the second law of thermodynamics that interests us most, and in the application of the laws of thermodynamics to cultural systems we have one of the most illuminating and profound interpretations of cultural systems that is currently available to us. The extent to which the laws of thermodynamics have been applied to cultural systems is so far very limited and not well understood (cf. White 1959b, ch. 2 for an extensive discussion of energy and cultural development).

According to the second law of thermodynamics, the cosmos is running downhill, breaking down, moving toward maximum entropy, which is chaos. On our planet at least, there are systems that are moving in a direction opposite to that specified for the cosmos as a whole by the second law of thermodynamics. These systems are biological organisms. They exemplify a process which is a building-up process. The process of biological evolution is one that moves toward greater complexity, toward more order, toward more organization, toward higher concentrations of energy rather than diffusions of energy, so that biological systems are moving in a direction opposite to that specified by the second law of thermodynamics for the cosmos as a whole. This does not mean that biological organisms are an exception to the rule or that they negate or invalidate the second law of thermodynamics. As a matter of fact, it is only because our solar system, our sun in particular, is running down that biological systems can build up. Somewhere along the line the impact of solar radiation upon physical and chemical materials on our planet created syntheses that were capable of capturing energy from the sun and utilizing it, not only to maintain the organization produced by the impact of solar radiation, but also to develop further and more complicated systems. The ability to capture some energy is the ability to capture more and more energy. The process of life is a thermodynamic process in reverse, so to speak.

Cultural systems are of the same sort. This is not surprising since cultural systems are adjuncts of the biological systems that are human beings. Cultural systems are thermodynamic systems also; that is to say, they capture energy, transform it and put it to work. Everything that a sociocultural system does requires energy. One of the dimensions of a cultural system is the magnitude of energy that is harnessed and expended by it per capita per year. The phrase "per capita per year" must be added; otherwise the phrase "more energy" is not significant. A cultural system of 200 people would harness and use twice as much energy as a cultural system of 100 people, other things being equal. But the amount of energy harnessed per capita per year might very well be exactly the same in these two systems.

The function of culture is to serve the needs of man, inner and outer, to make life secure and enduring. This requires energy. Cultural systems must harness energy and put it to work in order to produce certain results. The whole evolution of cultural systems is greatly illuminated by considering it in terms of energy harnessed and put to work, in terms of the amount of energy harnessed per capita per year, and in terms of the ways and means with which this energy is harnessed and put to work. The degree of cultural development is measured by the amount of energy harnessed and put to work per capita per year, other things being equal. The history of the evolution of culture shows that, throughout the history of man and culture, the amount of energy harnessed and put to work has been increased, sometimes gradually, sometimes abruptly. In short, the evolutionary process has been characterized by revolution as well as evolution, by sudden and profound change as well as by slower and more gradual change.

The first cultural systems to exist had the *human organism* as the source of energy by means of which they were activated. It is cultural systems that harness energy, not man. The energy of the human organism was harnessed by the first cultural systems that existed. A review of sources of energy available to the earliest cultural systems would include fire, wind, and water, in addition to the human organism. The importance of fire has been extolled in myth and eulogized in popular and in some scientific accounts of the evolution of culture. Fire has of course been important; but many discussions of the importance of fire are greatly exaggerated. Fire was important in some places for warmth. It may have been used to frighten wild animals away from a camp during the night. It could be used for cooking. (However, although cooking may be beneficial in some cases, according to many nutritionists cooking is injurious to many foods. Just where a balance of these two effects of fire upon foods would lie is an unanswered question.) Fire becomes very important in the ceramic arts and in metallurgy. But these uses of fire as such are not culture-builders. Fire becomes a culture-builder, in our sense of the term, only when it is employed as a form of mechanical energy, to do work. When the work done by fire is the equivalent of work that could be done by human muscle, it is functioning as a culture-builder. On very primitive cultural levels we find some instances, such as, for example, in hollowing out tree trunks for canoes; but all are insignificant. And it was not the use of fire that brought culture to the level of metallurgy; something else, namely agriculture, did that and then fire made metallurgy possible.

The amount of energy derived from human organisms by the earliest cultural systems was very, very small per capita per year. The adult male man is capable of generating about 1/10 of a horsepower. But the amount of power per capita was much less than 1/10 h.p. because the presence of babies and children, women, the aged and the infirm reduced the average. We estimate roughly that these earliest cultural systems, with the human organism as virtually their only source of energy, had about 1/20 h.p. per capita, which was a very small amount when compared with the horsepower of some of our lawnmowers or motor scooters.

The kind of culture produced by the harnessing and utilization of energy is determined by the *magnitude* of the energy harnessed and put to work per capita per year. There is a direct relationship between the amount of energy and the kind of culture, i.e., the degree of cultural development. We have here the same situation as that involved in building a brick wall: the magnitude of the brick wall is proportional to the amount of energy expended. The bigger the wall, the more energy; the more energy, the bigger the wall. And so it is with culture, other things being equal. The cultures of human history that were built wholly by human energy were exceedingly primitive, crude, meager, and simple. The cultures of the aborigines of Australia are examples of very primitive cultures organized on a human energy basis. In some respects they are about as primitive as possible technologically and sociologically. They have virtually no property, no dwellings, very little clothing, no bow and arrow, and few utensils; and Australian social organization had, as its principal units, groups that are found even among prehuman primates: territorial groups and the family. These cultures were so limited that the aborigines could pick up everything they possessed and walk easily from one locality to another.

Mankind would have continued to live indefinitely in this condition (which the older anthropologists used to call "savagery") had not some means been found to increase the amount of energy harnessed per capita per year. Intelligence, or lack of it, had nothing to do with it. A genius had to run down a kangaroo just the same as a "dumbbell." A cultural system of geniuses which rested upon human energy, and which was activated by human energy, would fall within the limits set by energy derivable from human organisms. It is worth noting that to date 99 percent of man's career on this planet has been spent in the human energy era with subsistence based on wild foods, i.e. 990,000 of the approximately million years that have elapsed since man appeared.

At a time estimated as about 8,000 B.C., in certain parts of the Old World new means were found to harness more energy per capita per year. These were the arts of agriculture and animal husbandry (Fig. 5). Plants and animals are forms and magnitudes of energy, solar energy. Up until 1942, all cultural systems on this planet were activated wholly by solar energy in one form or another. Plants and animals were *exploited* not only after man began but before he appeared. But exploiting is one thing and controlling these energy resources is something else. The techniques of animal husbandry and agriculture are cultural means of laying hold of and controlling new forces of nature, solar energy in plant and animal form. This is no different from control over solar energy effected by hydroelectric plants. It is exactly the same sort of thing. Agriculture and animal husbandry increased the amount of energy harnessed per capita per year very greatly. It increased the productivity of human labor enormously. More food could be produced per unit of human labor. Therefore, as a consequence of the origin and development of agriculture and animal husbandry, there was a very great and rapid rise of cultures, a great increase in cultural development. This theory is amply supported by archaeological facts and historical records. During the long, long human-energy period of approximately 990,000 years cultural progress was very meager and very, very slow. And then, within a very few thousand years after agriculture and animal husbandry got started, there was an enormous development of cultures in Mesopotamia and the Nile Valley: little tribes became big tribes, confederations of tribes developed, then tribal organization was obliterated and states were created, and finally, empires appeared. All of the arts and crafts grew rapidly: large cities, gigantic architectural edifices and engineering projects, writing, astronomy, the beginning of sciences, and so on. Archaeological facts and historical records amply support the theory that when and as the amount of energy harnessed and put to work is rapidly and greatly increased, so will the culture grow and develop rapidly and greatly. The same process occurred at a somewhat later time in the New World in Peru and Middle America after the domestication of food.

Why did agriculture and animal husbandry begin when and where they

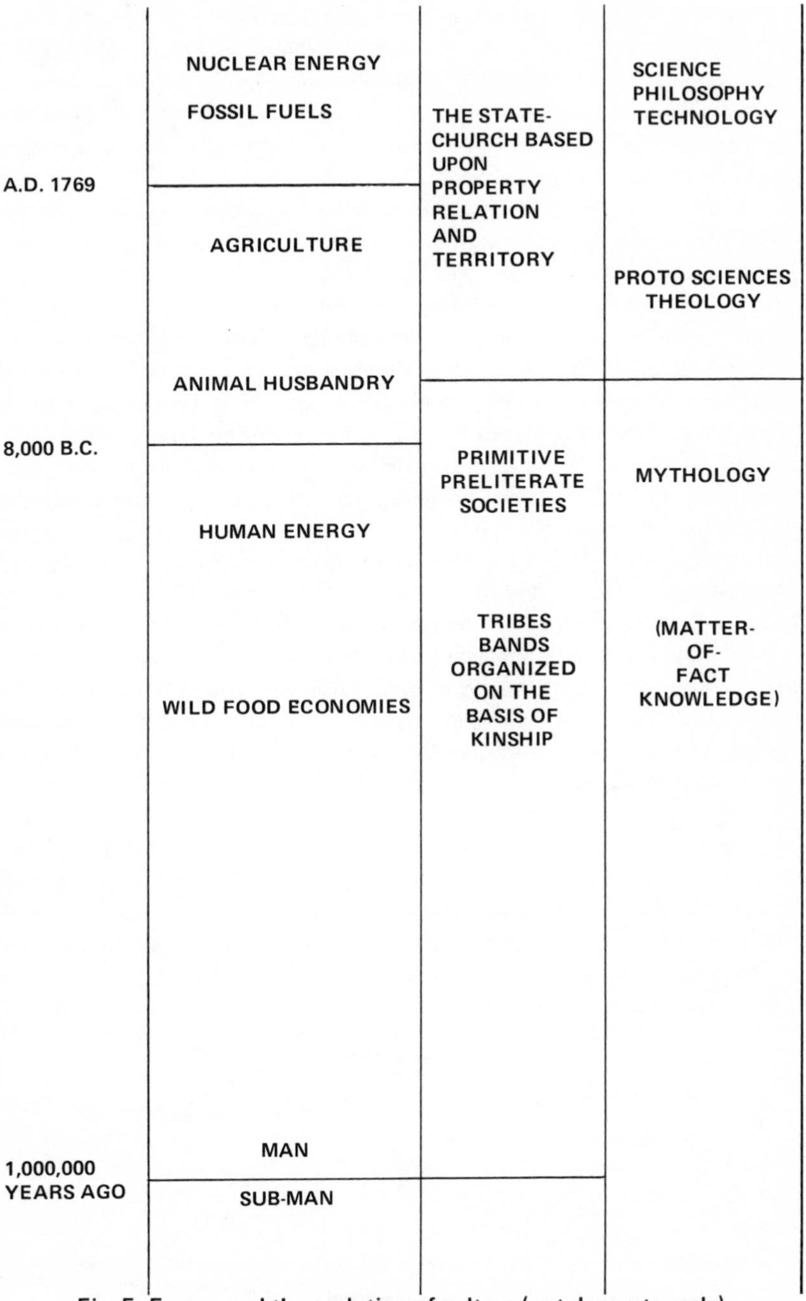

Fig. 5. Energy and the evolution of culture (not drawn to scale).

did? Briefly, the best explanation that science has to offer is that with the recession of the last great ice sheet a large part of central Asia became arid and uninhabitable, causing migration of people, who, moving into other areas, increased pressure upon the food supply, a pressure sufficient to transform mere exploitation in gathering and hunting into cultural control by means of animal husbandry and agriculture.

There was a period of great and rapid development after agriculture and animal husbandry began. But after a time the social, political, and economic systems affected the technological system so as to arrest development and progress and the curve of cultural development leveled off. Moreover, if cultural systems had continued to be founded solely upon agriculture and animal husbandry, further cultural development of significance would not have taken place for an indefinite period of time. Advances beyond peaks or levels reached in Mesopotamia and Egypt before the beginning of the Christian era would not have been superseded had not some way been found to increase the amount of energy harnessed per capita per year. The cultures of western and northern Europe were even cruder in the eighteenth century A.D. than some of the great cultures of the Bronze and Iron Age, as measured by meaningful criteria: size of city, size of architectural edifice, engineering knowledge (in some respects, though not all), and in some of the sciences. It is a very conservative statement to make that, had not some way to harness more energy per capita per year been devised by the cultural systems of western Europe in the eighteenth century, they would not have developed further to any significant degree for an indefinite period of time. Cultures cannot be built without energy.

Here again, of course, another way was found, namely, the harnessing of solar energy in the form of fossil fuels — coal, petroleum, and natural gas. Once again there was a tremendous leap forward in culture following the Fuel Revolution (Fig. 6). It placed the nations of western Europe and the United States in a position of preeminence and predominance in the whole world and made possible the great colonial empires of the late nineteenth century, as well as many other things.

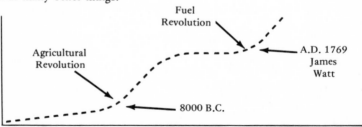

Fig. 6. The curve of cultural development (not drawn to scale).

Then in 1942, for the first time, a chain reaction in nuclear processes was achieved. Since that time nuclear reactors have been built and the possibility of their supplying a great amount of energy in the future seems to be very good.

Here, then, is the history of cultural development in terms of harnessing energy. No other theory or concept makes as intelligible, as understandable, how and why cultures have developed as this one does. It is the most illuminating and profound explanation that we have. Incidentally, the energy theory of cultural development was developed by physicists, primarily, and by chemists. Anthropologists have had little part in the development of this theory, and some of them have been very reluctant to accept it when it was made available to them.

To harness energy and put it to work, one must have means. These means are tools and machines, and the techniques with which they are used. The phrase "other things being equal" has been added here to almost every statement made about harnessing energy and putting it to work. It is necessary to add this phrase because, in actuality, other things never *are* equal. The tool (instrumental) factor is involved in technology just as the energy factor is. The concept of the energy theory of cultural development can be expressed by this formula: $E \times T = P$, where T is tools, E is energy, and P is the product in human goods and services produced by the expenditure of energy. This formula makes it clear that E can remain constant while T varies, in which case P would vary. Theoretically, of course, E and T can increase or decrease or remain constant, or they can vary inversely. They can vary in any mathematically possible way.

We now review the history of cultural development from the standpoint of energy and tools. Human energy was the first, and virtually the only, source of energy during the long early period, and the energy was put to work by means of tools. The tool factor was not a constant throughout these 990,000 years. Some progress was made in the development of tools. New tools were invented from time to time and old tools were improved. We know this from archaeological evidence (especially, of course, for more recent times). Thus, some cultural progress was possible and was achieved during this long period, not because of an increase in the amount of energy harnessed per capita per year, but because of an increase in the efficiency of the tools with which this energy was put to work.

The efficiency of a tool varies between 0 and 100 percent. The efficiency of a tool may be increased, but there is a limit beyond which a tool cannot be made more efficient. A perfect canoe paddle is one which would become less efficient if it were any longer or shorter, wider or narrower, heavier or lighter, or modified in any other way. It is also important to note that the increase in efficiency of a tool does not increase the amount of energy available for use. Increasing the efficiency of a tool increases the magnitude of the product of the expenditure of energy, but does not increase the *amount* of energy available for use. The amount of energy harnessed per capita per year during the early, wild food era remained a constant. Increasing the efficiency of the steam engine does not increase the amount of coal burned. Had the tool factor also remained constant during this early period, there would have been no cultural progress at all. But the amount of cultural progress that was possible was limited by the maximum efficiency of the tools used. When, or if, that maximum efficiency point was reached, cultural progress came to a stop.

. What was true with respect to tools prior to the Agricultural Revolution was valid after the advent of agriculture and animal husbandry. But the arts of domestication did not reach their limits of technological development by any means and have not done so yet; and this of course raises the question, "Why was technological progress in the arts of subsistence arrested?" The answer, which has already been suggested, is that the social, political, and economic systems curbed and finally arrested technological advance.

In the course of cultural development we find energy being derived from a number of different sources, and for certain purposes it is desirable to distinguish human energy from energy derived from nonhuman sources. This is desirable, or significant, because we are human beings. It is our welfare that culture in general is ministering to, and what is done to us is important to us. So a distinction between human energy and nonhuman energy becomes significant in our analysis of sources of energy throughout a million years of human history. One generalization we can make with respect to this distinction is that as culture evolves, the percentage of human energy, relative to the total amount harnessed, diminishes; that is to say, energy from other sources is added to human energy. This same idea could be expressed in another way, namely, that the productivity of human labor increases. With great increases in the amount of *total energy harnessed*, and with enormous *advances in the efficiency of the means* by which it is put to work, the productivity of human labor becomes enormous. We have now reached a high peak in this productivity with automated factories, which produce technological unemployment. We can now conceive of a new type of culture: a culture in which the amount of energy harnessed per capita per year is so great, and so is the efficiency of the means of putting it to work with electronic devices (which take the place of the human mind just as the steam engine took the place of human muscles) that human beings will be almost wholly emancipated from labor. This, of course, would (and in fact does) present problems.

Let us survey rather rapidly a correlation of the institutional and ideological components of cultural systems with the technological components. Just as we have a very long era of wild food, of human energy, so do we have a rather long era of what is commonly called "primitive society," i.e., society organized on the basis of kinship, motivated by principles of mutual aid and cooperation, and structured in clans, lineages, moieties, and tribes. We know of some cultural systems that possess well-developed animal husbandry or agriculture but are still organized on the basis of kinship and tribes. It took some time for the development of agriculture and animal husbandry to reach the point where this type of subsistence could no longer be accommodated by the institutions of tribe and clan. Animal husbandry and agriculture brought new forces, cultural forces, into being which eventually could no longer be accommodated, or contained, by tribes and clans. Consequently, tribal organization was destroyed, and as this took place, a new form of political structure was created, namely the state-church (cf. White 1959b).

But changes in social organization lag behind technological changes. The Fuel Revolution has not as yet displaced or replaced the state-church as a means of political organization and control (Fig. 5). But a political revolution is nevertheless evidently in the making. If civilization is not destroyed by warfare, but continues to grow and develop, there will undoubtedly be another political revolution and an entirely new type of society will be established. This new type will most likely be one in which the church-state will be nonexistent: a society in which there will be an administration of *things* rather than the governing of men; and again society will be organized on the basis of personal relations rather than property relations. Property rights will be subordinated to human rights and human welfare.

This leads us to the economic component of cultural systems. During the long era of primitive society, economic systems were virtually identical with social systems, animated by the same principles of mutual aid and cooperation. Property rights were subordinated to human rights and human relationships. As a matter of fact, the economic systems of many primitive societies correspond closely with their kinship systems. Kinship systems are one of the most fascinating aspects of primitive cultures. A body of kindred is a group of people who are related to one another by ties of consanguinity and affinity (by blood and marriage). A kinship system is an organized form of behavior in terms of mutual aid and cooperation. In primitive cultures, much, if not all, of the economic system was identified with kinship. The kinship systems provided primitive peoples with a remarkable kind of social security. All one's relatives were obligated to help him. Everyone was obligated to share what he had with anyone else in times of need. This of course meant placing human welfare and human rights above property rights.

The Agricultural Revolution transformed the economic systems of primitive cultures as it transformed the political systems. Primitive society was characterized by liberty, equality, and fraternity. This slogan raised so eloquently in the French Revolution was raised because modern society is characterized by the absence of liberty, equality, and fraternity. People are not free; they are in bondage of one sort or another from chattel slavery to "wage slavery." Exploitation, competition, and conflict characterize modern society, rather than cooperation and mutual aid. One of the most striking differences between the economic system of primitive society and that of civil society is this: in primitive society there was communal living, mutual sharing, what is mine is thine; people received and consumed things simply because they were human beings.

There was also, of course, some private, personal property in primitive society. Most of it was personal belongings, although in some instances there was that which might be called private property in resources of nature. That is to say, a family or clan might own a piece of land or a tree or some such. But here the term "own" does not mean what it does in our society, i.e., it was not absolute ownership but rather the right to use. No one and no group in primitive society was ever excluded from free access to the resources of nature. Freedom to exploit the resources of nature means freedom and equality, and the kinship organization provides the fraternity.

In civil society, a small dominant group exercises a monopoly over the resources of nature and controls the exploitation of it. This group controls it in such a way that the masses of the population live in relative poverty, whereas the small dominant minority possesses or controls vast wealth. If and when cultural development reaches the point of another revolution, the best prediction is that a kind of relationship will be established again in which all human beings will have free and equal access to the resources of nature. "...the next higher plan of society...will be a revival, in a higher form, of the liberty, equality and fraternity of the ancient gentes." (Morgan 1964:467. A facsimile of the original statement in Morgan's handwriting appears as the frontispiece of this edition of *Ancient Society*.) Production will be for use and consumption in terms of need. This is not just a wish or hope or fancy. A society of this sort was realized long ago. The human race originally lived in a society without the foundation of private property, for 99 percent of its career.

Turning now to the ideological aspect of culture, we have what we call "matter of fact knowledge." The matter of fact knowledge of primitive society was not fully expressed in language. For example, considerable knowledge is needed in order to make good pottery. But primitive peoples had no intellectual tradition about how to make pottery, although they did have a lot of matter of fact knowledge. They knew and understood the properties of almost everything in their habitat. They understood many physical, mechanical, and chemical processes and principles, and could do a great many things that require knowledge and skill. But most of this knowledge did not constitute an overt, verbalized, intellectual tradition. It was transmitted by example rather than with language. In contrast, in mythology (that is, with regard to questions that could not be answered realistically) there was a very great tradition. Myths of all kinds explained how the world came to be, or how it was shaped, who put up the sun, the moon, and the stars, the origin of animals, why the badger has a white streak on his forehead, the first homicide, the institution of clans, the origin of fire, the acquisition of corn, and so on (Fig. 5). Primitive peoples have answers to all the important questions, which is, strictly speaking, omniscience.

From the standpoint of the achievement of civilization intellectually, omniscience is one of the greatest obstacles to the achievement of a civilized mind. The achievement of pure, uncontaminated, unadulterated ignorance by science, the insistence upon not-knowing when we do not know, and the defending of this ignorance with vigor and determination, is what characterizes the modern civilized mind and distinguishes it from all of its predecessors.

Theology differs from mythology in two respects. Theology is fundamentally like mythology in being supernaturalistic. About the only meaningful distinction which can be made between mythology and theology is that the latter is more systematized, has been reduced to writing, and is in the custody of a special class called priests.

Mythology became transformed into theology during the Agricultural Revolution. The body of matter of fact knowledge, which had been in existence for ages, was systematized in the hands of specialists into the proto-sciences: astrology-astronomy, anatomy, chemistry, physics, mechanics, medicine, etc. An exceptional development of thought took place among the ancient Greeks in which rational thought and naturalism were applied to thinking about man and society as well as to the biological and inanimate world. But, with the decline of the great Bronze and Iron Age cultures, western Europe lay dormant under a thick blanket of supernaturalism for centuries. Slowly, step by step, rational thought, empirical investigations, grew until, by 1859 and the publication of *The Origin of Species,* the tide had turned. Science had free rein, although theological opposition was not wholly eliminated, by any means. However, the trend in Western culture has been, and still is, towards increased naturalistic and scientific ideology.

References Cited

Benedict, R. 1934. *Patterns of culture.* Boston: Houghton Mifflin.

————. 1942. "Primitive freedom." *Atlantic Monthly* 169:756-63.

Bidney, D. 1944. "On the concept of culture and some cultural fallacies." *American Anthropologist* 46:30-44.

Boas, F. 1938. *The mind of primitive man.* New York: Macmillan Co.

Brinton, D. 1900. Brinton memorial meeting. Philadelphia: American Philosophical Society.

Darwin, C. 1871. *The descent of man.* London: John Murray.

————. 1888. *The life and letters of Charles Darwin.* Francis Darwin, ed. 2 vols. New York: D. Appleton & Co.

Durkheim, E. 1938. *The rules of the sociological method.* Chicago: University of Chicago Press.

Goldenweiser, A. A. 1914. "The social organization of the Indians of North America." *Journal of American Folklore* 27:411-36.

————. 1921. "Four phases of anthropological thought." Proceedings, Sixteenth Annual Meeting of the American Sociological Society.

————. 1922. *Early civilization.* New York: A. A. Knopf.

————. 1924. "Anthropological theories of political origins." In *A History of Political Theories.* C. E. Merriam and H. E. Barnes, eds. New York: Macmillan Co.

————. 1925. "Cultural anthropology." In *History and Prospects of the Social Sciences.* H. E. Barnes, ed. New York: A. A. Knopf.

————. 1925. "Diffusionism and the American school of historical ethnology." *American Journal of Sociology* 31:19-38.

————. 1927. "Anthropology and psychology." In *The Social Sciences and Their Interrelations.* W. F. Ogburn and A. Goldenweiser, eds. Boston: Houghton Mifflin.

————. 1931. "Evolution, Social." *Encyclopaedia of the Social Sciences.* New York.

————. 1937. *Anthropology.* New York: Appleton-Century-Crofts.

Hallowell, A. I. 1945. "Sociopsychological aspects of acculturation." In *Science of Man in the World Crisis*. R. Linton, ed. New York: Columbia University Press.

Herskovits, M. J. 1948. *Man and his works*. New York: A. A. Knopf.

Kardiner, A., and E. Preble. 1961. *They studied man*. Cleveland: World Publishing Co.

Keller, H. 1903. *The story of my life*. New York: Doubleday, Page & Co.

Kellogg, W. N., and L. A. Kellogg. 1933. *The ape and the child*. New York: McGraw-Hill.

Klemm, G. 1843-1852. *Allgemeine Culturgeschichte der Menschheit*. 10 vols. Leipzig: Leubner.

————. 1844-1855. *Allgemeine Culturwissenschaft*. 2 vols. Leipzig: Leubner.

Köhler, W. 1926. *The mentality of apes*. New York and London: Harcourt Brace.

Kroeber, A. L. 1917. "The superorganic." *American Anthropologist* 19: 163-213.

Kroeber, A. L., and C. Kluckhohn. 1952. *Culture: a critical review of concepts and definitions*. Papers of the Peabody Museum of American Archeology and Ethnology 47:1. Cambridge, Mass.

Laufer, B. 1918. Review of Robert H. Lowie's *Culture and Ethnology*. *American Anthropologist* 20:87-91.

Lévi-Strauss, C. 1949. "Histoire et ethnologie." *Revue de Metaphysique et de Morale* 58:363-91.

Linton, R. 1936. *The study of man*. New York: D. Appleton-Century.

————. 1945. *The cultural background of personality*. New York: D. Appleton-Century.

Lowie, R. H. 1917. *Culture and ethnology*. New York: D. C. McMurtrie.

————. 1920. *Primitive society*. New York: Boni and Liveright.

————. 1936. "Cultural anthropology: a science." *American Journal of Sociology* 42:301-20.

Lynd, R. S. 1939. *Knowledge for what?* Princeton: Princeton University Press.

Malinowski, B. 1941. "Man's culture and man's behavior." *Sigma Xi Quarterly* 29:182-96.

Marx, K. 1904. *Critique of political economy*. Chicago: International Library Publishing Co.

Mead, M., and R. Bunzel, eds. 1960. *The golden age of American anthropology*. New York: George Braziller.

Morgan, L. H. 1959. *The Indian journals 1859-62*. Ed. with an introduction by L. A. White. Ann Arbor: University of Michigan Press.

————. 1964. *Ancient society*. L. A. White, ed. Cambridge, Mass.: Belknap Press of Harvard University (original 1877).

Murdock, G. P. 1949. *Social structure.* New York: Macmillan Co.

————. 1951. "British social anthropology." *American Anthropologist* 53:465-73.

Newcomb, W.W., Jr. 1950. "A re-examination of the causes of Plains warfare." *American Anthropologist* 52:317-30.

Ogburn, W. F. 1922. *Social change.* New York: B. W. Huebach.

Ogburn, W. F., and D. Thomas. 1922. "Are inventions inevitable?" *Political Science Quarterly* 37:83-98.

Osgood, C. 1940. *Ingalik material culture.* Yale University Publications in Anthropology 22.

————. 1951. "Culture: its empirical and non-empirical character." *Southwestern Journal of Anthropology* 7:202-14.

Pitt-Rivers, A. H. L. 1906. *The evolution of culture and other essays.* J. L. Myres, ed. Oxford: Clarendon Press.

Radcliffe-Brown, A. R. 1940. "On social structure." *Journal of the Royal Anthropological Institute of Great Britain and Ireland* 70:1-12.

————. 1957. *A natural science of society.* Glencoe, Ill.: Free Press.

Radin, P. 1939. "The mind of primitive man." *The New Republic* 98: 300-303.

Reichard, G. 1938. "Social life." In *General Anthropology.* Franz Boas, ed. New York: D. C. Heath & Co.

Roheim, G. 1943. *The origin and function of culture.* Nervous and Mental Disease Monographs. New York.

Sapir, E. 1920. Review of Robert H. Lowie's *Primitive Society. The Freeman* 1:377-79.

————. 1930. "Southern Paiute, a Shoshonean language." *Proceedings of the American Academy of Arts and Sciences* 65:1-296.

————. 1932. "Cultural anthropology and psychiatry." *Journal of Abnormal and Social Psychology* 27:229-42.

Spencer, H. 1852. "The development hypothesis." *The Leader* III.

————. 1896. *Principles of sociology.* New York: D. Appleton & Co.

Spiro, M. E. 1951. "Culture and personality." *Psychiatry* 14:19-47.

Strong, W. D. 1953. "Historical approach in anthropology." In *Anthropology Today.* A. L. Kroeber, ed. Chicago: University of Chicago Press.

Taylor, W. W. 1948. *A study of archaeology.* American Anthropological Association Memoir 69.

Tylor, E. B. 1871. *Primitive culture.* London: J. Murray.

————. 1881. *Anthropology.* London: J. Murray.

————. 1893. "On the Tasmanians as representative of paleolithic man." *Journal of the Royal Anthropological Institute of Great Britain and Ireland* 23:141-52.

White, L. A. (ed.) 1937. *Extracts of Lewis Henry Morgan's European travel journal.* Rochester Historical Society Publications 16. Rochester, N. Y.

White, L. A. 1939. "A problem in kinship terminology." *American Anthropologist* 41:566-73.

_____. 1948. "The definition and prohibition of incest." *American Anthropologist* 50:416-35.

_____. 1949. "Ethnological theory." In *Philosophy for the Future.* R. W. Sellers, V. J. McGill, and M. Farber, eds. New York: Macmillan Co.

_____. 1959a. "The concept of culture." *American Anthropologist* 61:227-51.

_____.1959b. *The evolution of culture.* New York: McGraw-Hill Book Co.

_____. 1960. "Four stages in the evolution of minding." In *Evolution after Darwin II, The Evolution of Man.* S. Tax, ed. Chicago: University of Chicago Press.

_____. 1962. "Symboling: a kind of behavior." *Journal of Psychology* 53:311-17.

_____. 1966. *The social organization of ethnological theory.* Rice University Studies 52.

_____. 1968. "Culturology." In *International Encyclopedia of the Social Sciences.*

_____. 1969. *The science of culture,* rev. ed. New York: Farrar, Straus & Giroux.

Williams, J. J. 1936. "Boas and American ethnologists." *Thought* 11:194-209.

Wissler, C. 1929. *Introduction to social anthropology.* New York: Holt.

Zipf, G. K. 1949. *Human behavior and the principle of least effort.* Cambridge, Mass.: Addison-Wesley Press.

# Additional Readings

The following bibliography was designed with three objectives in mind: (1) to amplify points made in the text; (2) to provide the reader with sources of information about specific cultures and aspects of culture which are referred to in the text but not described or defined; and (3) to select works which are generally available. Works listed in References Cited are not repeated here.

The Basis of Culture: The Symbol

Cowles, J. T. 1937. *Food tokens as incentives for learning.* Comparative Psychology Monographs 16, no. 5.

Ferster, C. B. 1964. "Arithmetic behavior in chimpanzees." *Scientific American* 120.

Wolfe, J. B. 1936. *Effectiveness of token-rewards for chimpanzees.* Comparative Psychology Monographs 12, no. 5.

Man and Culture

Coon, C. S. 1948. *Reader in general anthropology.* New York: Henry Holt & Co.

Barton, R. F. 1956. *The half-way sun; life among the headhunters of the Philippines.* New Haven: reprinted by the Human Area Relations Files.

Day, C. 1948. "This simian world." In *The Best of Clarence Day.* New York: A. A. Knopf.

Devore, I., ed. 1965. *Primate behavior: field studies of monkeys and apes.* New York: Holt, Rinehart & Winston.

Forde, C. D. 1949. *Habitat, economy and society; a geographical introduction to ethnology.* New York: reprinted by Dutton.

Freuchen, P. 1961. *Book of the Eskimos.* 3rd ed. Greenwich, Conn.: reprinted by Fawcett World.

Jay, P., ed. 1968. *Primates: studies in adaptation and variability.* New York: Holt, Rinehart & Winston.

Lawick-Goodall, J. 1971. *In the shadow of man.* Boston: Houghton Mifflin.

Service, E. P. 1971. *Profiles in ethnology,* rev. ed. New York: Harper & Row.
White, L. A. 1942. "On the use of tools by primates." *Journal of Comparative Psychology* 34:369-74. Indianapolis: reprinted in Bobbs-Merrill reprint series.

Man, Cultural Variation, and the Concept of Culture

Kelso, A. J. 1970. *Physical anthropology, an introduction.* Philadelphia: Lippincott.
Lockwood, W. W. 1954. *The economic development of Japan: growth and structural change, 1868-1938.* Princeton: Princeton University.
White, L. A. 1935. *The pueblo of Santo Domingo, New Mexico.* American Anthropological Association Memoir 43.
————. 1942. *The pueblo of Santa Ana, New Mexico.* American Anthropological Association Memoir 60.
Wissler, C. 1923. Man and culture. New York: Thomas Y. Crowell.

Other Conceptions of Culture

Cohen, M. R. 1953. *Reason and nature: an essay on the meaning of scientific method.* 2nd ed. Glencoe, Ill.: Free Press.
White, L. A. 1959. "The concept of culture." *American Anthropologist* 61: 227-51. Indianapolis: reprinted in Bobbs-Merrill reprint series.

Culturology

Dole, G. E. and R. L. Carneiro, eds. 1960. *Essays in the science of culture in honor of Leslie A. White.* New York: Thomas Y. Crowell.
Schusky, E. L. 1965. *Manual for kinship analysis: a study in anthropological method.* New York: Holt, Rinehart & Winston.
Wilder, R. L. 1968. *Evolution of mathematical concepts: an elementary study.* New York: John Wiley & Sons.

Culture as System

Halloway, R. L., et al. 1967. "War: the anthropology of armed conflict and aggression." *Natural History* 76, no. 10.
Radcliffe-Brown, A. R. 1952. *Structure and function in primitive society.* Glencoe, Ill.: Free Press.

History of the Theory of Cultural Evolution

Elkin, A. P. 1954. *The Australian aborigines.* Foreword by M. Mead. Garden City, N. Y.: Natural History Press.
Herskovits, M. J. 1965. "Papers in honor of M. J. Herskovits." *Current Anthropology* 6, no. 1.

Lowie, R. H. 1937. *History of ethnological theory.* New York: Farrar & Rinehart.

Morgan, L. H. 1962. *League of the Ho-de-no-sau-nee or Iroquois.* W. N. Fenton, ed. New York: Corinth Books.

Sahlins, M. D., and E. P. Service, eds. 1960. *Evolution and culture.* Ann Arbor: University of Michigan Press.

How Culture Evolved

Adams, R. M. 1966. *Evolution of urban society: early Mesopotamia and pre-Hispanic Mexico.* Chicago: Aldine.

Childe, V. G. 1946. *What happened in history.* New York: Pelican.

Tylor, E. B. 1960. *Anthropology.* Abridged and with an introduction by L. A. White. Ann Arbor: University of Michigan.

Vaillant, G. C. 1962. *Aztecs of Mexico: origin, rise and fall of the Aztec nation.* Revised by S. B. Vaillant. New York: Pelican.

Willey, G. R. 1960. "New World Prehistory." *Science* 131. Indianapolis: reprinted in Bobbs-Merrill reprint series.